Hare

Animal
Series editor: Jonathan Burt

Already published

Crow
Boria Sax

Ant
Charlotte Sleigh

Tortoise
Peter Young

Cockroach
Marion Copeland

Dog
Susan McHugh

Oyster
Rebecca Stott

Bear
Robert E. Bieder

Bee
Claire Preston

Rat
Jonathan Burt

Snake
Drake Stutesman

Falcon
Helen Macdonald

Whale
Joe Roman

Parrot
Paul Carter

Tiger
Susie Green

Salmon
Peter Coates

Fox
Martin Wallen

Fly
Steven Connor

Cat
Katharine M. Rogers

Peacock
Christine E. Jackson

Cow
Hannah Velten

Swan
Peter Young

Shark
Dean Crawford

Rhinoceros
Kelly Enright

Moose
Kevin Jackson

Duck
Victoria de Rijke

Horse
Elaine Walker

Elephant
Daniel Wylie

Eel
Richard Schweid

Ape
John Sorenson

Penguin
Stephen Martin

Snail
Peter Williams

Owl
Desmond Morris

Pigeon
Barbara Allen

Lion
Deirdre Jackson

Camel
Robert Irwin

Forthcoming

Spider
Katja and Sergiusz Michalski

Pig
Brett Mizelle

Chicken
Annie Potts

Wolf
Gary Marvin

Butterfly
Matthew Brower

Sheep
Philip Armstrong

Octopus
Helen Tiffin

Flea
Karin Barton

Giraffe
Mark Williams

Beetle
Adam Dodd

Donkey
Jill Bough

Bat
Judith Halberstam

Hare

Simon Carnell

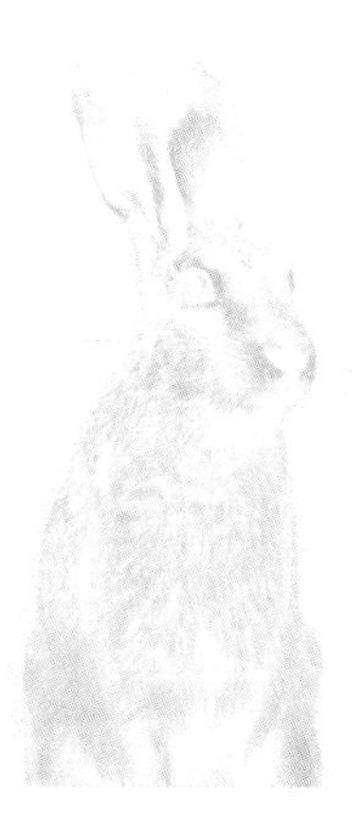

REAKTION BOOKS

For Erica Segre, and for Aurora and Gabriel Segre Carnell

Published by
REAKTION BOOKS LTD
33 Great Sutton Street
London EC1V 0DX, UK
www.reaktionbooks.co.uk

First published 2010

Printed and bound in China by Eurasia

British Library Cataloguing in Publication Data
Carnell, Simon, 1962–
Hare. – (Animal)
1. Hares 2. Hares in art
I. Title
599.3'28

ISBN: 978 1 86189 431 1

Contents

TVTE LEPVS ES ET PVLPAMENTVM QVAERIS
3
1
2
XX
LEPVS DORMIT.

1 *Lagographia Curiosa*: The Natural and Unnatural History of the Hare

Even allowing for the degree to which works of pre-eighteenth-century natural history contain mistaken and eccentric material regarding most animals (the mole has only one drop of blood in its body; swallows nest underwater in winter; the sloth takes a month to climb a tree, and so on), the hare receives some remarkably colourful and extensive treatment in such works. Aelian, in his *On Animals*, maintained that male as well as female hares gave birth, and that the hare 'sleeps with its body alone while it continues to see with its eyes . . . enjoying this advantage over all other animals'.[1] Aristotle both exaggerated the hare's capacity for rapid increase, and in a passage in *On the Generation of Animals* argued that the hare's peculiar reproductive power was related to its 'hairiness': 'for the quantity of their hair is excessive . . . hairiness is a sign of abundance of residual matter, wherefore among men also the hairy are given to sexual intercourse and have much more semen than the smooth'.[2] He also believed that hares do not give birth to their young 'all together and at one time, but bring them forth over as many days as the circumstances of each case may require'.[3] Though not a work of natural history as such, Xenophon's influential *Cynegeticus*, the earliest extant hunting treatise, remarks of the hare's eyesight that 'its very fleetness of foot contributes largely towards its dim-sightedness. It can only take a rapid glance at things in passing,

Types of hare, with squirrel, by Georg Hoefnagel, from *Terra: Animalia Quadrupedia et Reptilia*, c. 1575–80.

and then off before perceiving what the particular object is.' When awake, according to Xenophon, 'it keeps blinking its eyelids, but when asleep the eyelids remain wide open and motionless and the eyes rigidly fixed'.[4]

Pliny writes in his *Natural History* that alpine hares turn white because they eat snow; that 'a deaf hare will sooner feed and grow fat, than another that heareth', and reports the popular belief that hare flesh 'causeth them that feed upon it to look fair, lovely, & gracious, for a week together afterwards'.[5] He also includes details of how to use hare *materia* – blood, the womb, faeces, unborn leverets – in order, respectively, to boost male reproductive power; cause a male rather than a female child to be conceived; keep the breasts of a young virgin firm; make a menopausal woman fertile again. Drawing on the work of Dioscorides and others, such uses of the hare in 'physicke' were much multiplied and elaborated upon by the likes of the thirteenth-century monk Albertus Magnus, who despite the hare's reputation for hyper-sexuality, and the frequently sexual nature of its proto-medicinal uses, was convinced that it was an animal both 'cold-blooded and cold-hearted'.[6]

'Sleepless' hare, from Conrad Gessner's *Historia Animalium*, 1551–8.

Edward Topsell in his *History of Four-footed Beasts* (1607) reports the widespread opinion that the hare is 'one year male, and another female'. Topsell believed that it 'seldom looketh forward' when fleeing, and that its lips continually move, 'sleeping and waking'. He also gives a peculiar twist to the belief that it sleeps open-eyed, by asserting that 'when they watch they shut their eyes, and when they sleep they open them'. As for its exceptional speed, he thought that it was aided by one forward-stretching ear which it used 'like a sail' when fleeing, for 'the ears of this Beast are like Angels wings, Ships sails, and rowing Oars, to help her in her flight'.[7] He concludes his account with several pages of material, much of it backed up with authority from learned authors, on how virtually every part of the hare can be used medicinally: for the treatment of everything from epilepsy, baldness, bladder stones, ruptured bowels, memory loss and deafness – to the bite of a venomous spider or wound from a poisoned arrow; stalled labour; 'cankers' and 'inflamation of a Womans secrets after their child birth'. In order to underscore the proven nature of this material, he gives short shrift in passing to the fact that 'the secrets and stones of Hares are given to Men and Women to make them apter to copulation and conception, but this opinion hath no other ground beside the fecundity of the beast that beareth them'. There is hardly a creature that did not figure in some way in pre-modern medicine, but William Cogan in his *Haven of Health* (1596) is unequivocal about the particular efficacy of hares: 'no beast, be it never so great, is profitable to so many and so diverse uses in Physicke as the hare'.[8] Or as John Johnston put it, in his *A Description of the Nature of Four-footed Beasts* (1657), there is 'no part almost of the Hare that is not usefull' in 'Phisick', 'even the very excrements'.[9]

Medicinal uses of the hare continued throughout the seventeenth century and beyond. To such an extent, in fact, that

From *Materia medica* by Pedanius Dioscorides, in a 16th-century Italian translation, in illustration of his passage 'on the marine and terrestrial hare'.

information about them outweighs the natural history contained in the only pre-nineteenth-century monographs on hares: *Lagographia* by Wolfgang Waldung (1619) and Franz Christian Paullini's *Lagographia Curiosa* (1691). Even Francis Bacon, the scourge of natural histories 'fraught with much fabulous matter, a great part not only untried, but notoriously untrue',[10] gave credence to the idea that the brains of hares, when roasted and marinated in wine, could 'strengthen the memory'.[11]

In seeking to dispense with 'vulgar errors' concerning hares, in his *Pseudodoxia Epidemica* (1646), Sir Thomas Browne takes up the vexed question of their sex-changing, and concludes that they *do* change their sex, 'but sometimes, and not in that vicissitude or annual alteration as is presumed'.[12] They can do so, according to Browne, from female to male, but not back again, or from female to male at all. Browne also believed, like Aristotle before him, that from certain peculiarities of the hare's anatomy 'there ensueth a necessity of retrocopulation', with the male and female facing in opposite directions when mating. Browne has extricated himself from the tradition of associating the hare with 'lustfulness', but cannot resist a piece of moralizing by way of conclusion, albeit one which turns the usual association on its head. Hares copulate this way out of necessity: only humans have devised a variety of sexual positions for their sinful delectation.

By the time we reach the *Histoire naturelle, générale et particulière* (1749–1788) of the Comte de Buffon, one of the key works of popularizing natural history to come out of the Enlightenment, the belief about gender-shifting in hares has been dropped, along with much else besides. Though not the idea that they sleep with open eyes and steer with their ears – or that they are the fastest land mammal. And even here the history of speculation about the sexuality of hares takes an odd turn, under the guise and in the name of close and 'scientific' observation. For Buffon, hares are 'as equally lascivious as they are fertile. The glans of the clitoris is prominent, and nearly as large as that of the male penis.'[13] This super-sexed female hare is also said by him to be in possession of *two* uteri.

In his widely read and reprinted *History of Animated Nature* (1774), a work heavily indebted to Buffon's, Oliver Goldsmith omits this passage due, one suspects, to politeness rather than superior knowledge, and suffuses his account of the hare with an emphatic 'period' empathy. For Goldsmith it is 'pursued and persecuted on every side', 'the most persecuted, and the most timorous of creatures'. Hares 'without being enemies to any, are preyed upon by all'. Only in conclusion does he succumb to what Browne would have termed a 'vulgar error', by remarking in passing that 'some have been seen with horns, though these but rarely'.[14] Horned hares may have been rarely seen, but their existence was credited in Europe for five centuries, and a German edition of Buffon includes a coloured engraving of a hare with a magnificent set of miniature antlers.[15] Illustrations of horned hares also appear in Gessner and Johnston, in George Hoefnagel's *Animalia Quadrupedia et Reptilia* (1575) and in Gaspar Schott's *Physica Curiosa* (1662). A horned hare's skull is included in a description of items exhibited in 'Tradescant's Ark' (the first museum for the paying public in London), along with a mermaid's hand, dragon's egg, and piece of the 'True Cross'.

Such examples could be further multiplied. Certain premodern naturalists give a version of the idea that the hare is 'one of the most melancholicke beasts that is', and it is occasionally added that it can temporarily cure itself of this melancholy by seeking out and eating wild succory, or by just sitting under it.[16] Robert Burton, in his *Anatomy of Melancholy* (1621), says that eating hare flesh will not only cause 'fearful dreams' but 'breed incubus'; Johnston that it will cause 'grosse blood'.[17] Hares eat mice and have a particular liking for grapes. They will climb trees to evade capture, and only ever run in the direction of the wind. They never drink, 'but content themselves with the dew'. You can tell their age by counting 'the clefts in their dung'. They can not only predict the weather, but have 'certaine little bladders filled with matter' which they anoint their bodies with to make them waterproof before rain. There is a type of hare in North Carolina which plays host between its skin and flesh to a 'maggot' which turns in due course into a spectacularly beautiful butterfly. Female hares are so apt to conceive that even unborn leverets can become pregnant. There is a type of locally confined hare with two livers, one of which gradually disappears if it is transported from its native ground.[18]

In an otherwise brief, sober and accurate account of the hare, in his *General History of Quadrupeds* (1790), Thomas Bewick writes of an 'Alpine hare' in Tartary which harvests and stores herbs. This passage clearly demonstrates the survival into the eighteenth and even nineteenth centuries of peculiar 'observations' of the hare:

> In autumn great numbers assemble together, and collect vast quantities of the finest herbs, which, when dried, they form into pointed ricks of various sizes; some of them four or five feet in height, and of proportionable bulk. These they place under the shelter of an overhanging rock, or pile around the trunks of trees. By this means, these industrious little animals lay up a stock of winter food, and wisely provide against the rigours of those stormy regions; otherwise, being prevented by the depth of the snow from quitting their retreats in quest of food, they must all inevitably perish.[19]

'Observation' is precisely what's in question here, for no hare exhibits in fact anything like this behaviour. The description is based upon an eye-witness account, just as Aelian's, two millennia before him, was got partly from a hunter who describes taking a living leveret out from inside the 'womb' of a male hare. Bewick, though, was hardly a stranger to familiarity with *native* species, and in his *Autobiography* traces the very beginning of his feeling for animals, and therefore of his interest in natural history, to a childhood incident in which he held a terrified hunted hare in his arms. In the above passage his admiration and sympathy for the creature has resulted in nothing less than the construction or conversion of it into a thrifty farmer, exhibiting qualities of intelligence and even morality. Qualities which make it an unsuitable candidate (and this, I think, is the subtext) to be torn to pieces in the chase. In this respect it also seems designed

Gehörnte Hasen. Tab. LI.

v. Büff. N. d. Vierf. T. III T.

Horned hares, from an 18th-century German edition of Buffon's *Histoire naturelle* . . . .

to counter a no more accurate or scientific remark of Buffon's: hares are less intelligent than their closest relatives, the rabbits, because the latter provide themselves with burrows whereas the former do not, remaining primitively 'unhoused'.

Several further examples of nineteenth- and early twentieth-century writing about hares, though not simple 'mistakes' as such, serve to demonstrate the extent to which scientific, cultural and even political concerns affected the ways in which they were observed and depicted, even after much 'fabulous' material relating to them had been definitively relegated to the status of historical curiosity. P. H. Gosse, in his *Natural History* (1862), digresses in his section on the hare in order to deliver a brief sermon on the inhumanity of hare-hunting, just as another eminent nineteenth-century naturalist, William MacGillivray, had done before him, but goes on to conclude with a passage very differently inflected than Goldsmith's, Bewick's or MacGillivray's. He paraphrases a recent article by Charles Waterton describing a 'battle' of two male hares, 'continued till one died upon the field, the conqueror continuing to strike his prostrate adversary, when incapable of further resistance, with pertinacious malice

Thomas Bewick's woodcut of a brown hare, from *A General History of Quadrapeds*, 1790.

and fury'.[20] Gosse's use of this account is no doubt motivated by a desire to bring the hare thoroughly into a period conception of nature 'red in tooth and claw', albeit an anti-Darwinian one. He does so here by turning it into something like one of the protagonists in a Victorian translation of the *Iliad* or *Aeneid*. Instead of the proverbially timid hare, we are given heroic combatants upon the 'field' of battle. The wounded Hector may have compared himself to a lion insulted by hares, but Gosse's hares are capable of killing each other with leonine – or human – ferocity.

Darwin himself used the same exaggerated account of belligerent hares in *The Descent of Man* (1871), albeit rinsed of its purple prose; employing the hare as the first example of how, with mammals, 'the male appears to win the female much more through the law of battle than through the display of his charms. The most timid animals, not provided with any special weapons for fighting, engage in desperate conflicts during the season of love. Two male hares have been seen to fight until one was killed.'[21] The *Letters* bear witness to a point concerning hares which is of greater significance. In an important work which argued for the fixity of species, Georges Cuvier had used as an example the fact that hares do not interbreed with rabbits. No wonder, then, that Darwin was intrigued by contemporary experiments claiming to have produced hare–rabbit crosses or 'leporines' ('most curious, if true'), and in 1866 was sent an article by the fellow-travelling evolutionist Geoffroy Saint-Hilaire making precisely such a claim. Darwin was ultimately sceptical, and rightly so, for there must have been something fundamentally amiss with these 'experiments': hares have 42 chromosomes, rabbits 44. Though very differently motivated, those supporting the existence of leporines were giving credence to a creature as actually impossible and fabulous as the horned hare.[22]

Lepus europaeus (brown hare), from Archibald Thorburn's *British Mammals*, 1920–21.

One final example brings another chimerical *Lepus* into being, as it were: the anarchist hare. Naturalists such as Ernst Haeckel were quick to explore the reactionary political implications of Darwin's major work. The anarcho-communist Peter Kropotkin, in his *Mutual Aid: A Factor of Evolution* (1902), set out to contest conceptions of a perpetual, selfish and bloody war between and within species by giving a thoroughgoing account of their co-operations. When he reaches the hare, he is forced to concede the fact that it is relatively asocial, is 'not even endowed with intense parental feelings', and displays a marked antipathy towards its closest relative, the rabbit. Undeterred, however, it is

Ca.xlix.

at this point in his text that Kropotkin introduces the idea of the 'pleasures' animals in general derive from playing together, asserting in particular that 'our common hares . . . cannot live without coming together for play'. To back this up he quotes a contemporary hare expert who testifies to the fact that they are such 'passionate players' they have even been known to take an approaching fox for a playmate. What happens next to the hare is passed over in silence, in this almost subliminal reference to a pre-Fall or Golden Age. Kropotkin concludes with an ingenious explanation of the antipathy between hares and rabbits. Hares are 'passionate, eminently individualist'; rabbits 'placid, quiet and submissive': 'their tempers are too widely different not to be an obstacle to friendship'. Far from contradicting the general political argument with which he frames his natural history, then, the hare turns out, like Kropotkin, to be nothing less than a committed anarchist – with a natural scorn for the bourgeois conformism of the rabbit with its 'family life . . . entirely built upon the image of the old patriarchal family'.[23]

Animals, as Lévi-Strauss once famously remarked, are 'good to think'.[24] I have begun with the above material not in order to ridicule the inaccuracies of fact and emphasis of early natural historians, for accounts of the hare in these works also include observations which are remarkably accurate, and some of the mistakes can be seen to be based upon real insights. Nor do I intend merely to succumb to their quaintness and charm, though Topsell's hare in flight has the liveliness of a piece of folk art, and is not simply cancelled out by the 'accuracy' of Cuvier, for whom the creature has become 'distinguished by its long ears, short tail, hind-feet much longer than the fore'.[25] Instead I intend to show that, in addition and even prior to the symbolic, mythological, folkloric, religious and otherwise poetic material that has been generated by the hare (the kind of

Three hares swimming in a river, from *Ortus Sanitatis*, by Arnaldus de Villanova, 1491.

'thinking with animals' that Lévi-Strauss had in mind), it is more or less constructed and 'thought with' rather than simply observed – even in works which aim to report it objectively. And to further demonstrate that, especially but by no means exclusively in the pre-eighteenth-century natural histories, there is a marked tendency to see hares as essentially strange, *unheimlich*, unique or exceptional. For here is a creature so acutely sentient that it even sleeps with its eyes open, but one that is also 'purblind'. A familiar beast native throughout Europe, but one which also occurs in a form which is no more subject to verification than the unicorn. A quintessential game and prey species which is familiar to huntsman and cook alike, but one which possesses healing powers almost supernatural in their variety and potency. A mammal which is so 'persecuted' that it seems hardly suited for survival, but one which has hermaphroditic or sex-changing capacities and powers of reproduction unique among

Child born with hare's ears, from *Monstrorum Historia* by Ulisse Aldrovandi (1642).

creatures that nurse their offspring. A small quadruped but one capable of outstripping all others for speed. The epitome of 'timidity' which is nevertheless capable of extreme violence. An exuberant and headlong athlete which is at the same time capable of experiencing and causing 'melancholy', and the kind of interiority that this concept implies. And so on.

Step only slightly outside the ill-defined boundaries of pre-eighteenth-century natural history writing, or delve further into some of the more obviously folkloric material included by some of the writers already quoted, and the case of the hare becomes even curiouser. According to Philostratus, not only the variously ingested and concocted body parts of dead hares but the mere *presence* of a live one could be medicinally efficacious: carry a live hare around a woman in labour and then release it and her parturition will be aided.[26] In his *Naturall Magick* Giambattista della Porta relates how hare fat burnt in a lamp will cause women in the room where it is positioned to throw off their clothes and 'run about naked'.[27] In his *Remaines of Gentillisme* John Aubrey relates the belief that if you whisper to a captive hare that it is about to be killed for food, the next morning you will find it dead, having killed itself.[28] Several of the writers quoted above, as well as della Porta, thought that hare-lips in children were caused by their mothers having looked at a hare when they were pregnant. Ulisse Aldrovandi, in his *Monstrorum Historia*, includes an illustration of a child born with the ears of a hare: *Infans auribus leporinis*.[29] There are directions for the use of material derived from hares in order not just to alleviate the medical conditions listed above but to prevent dogs from ever barking again and to promote artificial speed and even courage in humans. Some of the early medicinal uses of hares clearly owe more to magic than folk wisdom – or at any rate to symbolic thinking. One writer details how to make garters sewn with the skin of a young hare: 'No horse can long keep up with a man on foot who is furnished with those garters'.[30] And even the relatively respectable William Cogan – a practising medic – relates that 'the knee-bone of an Hare taken out alive and worne about the necke is excellent against Convulsion fitts'.[31]

Hares have also been associated with actual witchcraft, with witches believed to have used them as 'familiars', or to have been capable of transforming themselves into hares – a belief which found pseudo-forensic confirmation in the witch-trials, with bite marks on the bodies of women pursued by dogs when in the form of a hare being sufficient evidence to convict them of supernatural practices. One of the last women executed in England for witchcraft was convicted upon an eye-witness account of how she had seemed to change, when about to be caught by a pursuing hound, from a hare to a woman. Diseased hares can be found with irregular bony growths on their heads, thus providing a simple explanation of the horned hare myth. But these malformations hardly resemble the antlers of horned

Three vague and one legendary species of hare, from Anselme Desmarest's *Mammalogie*, 1820.

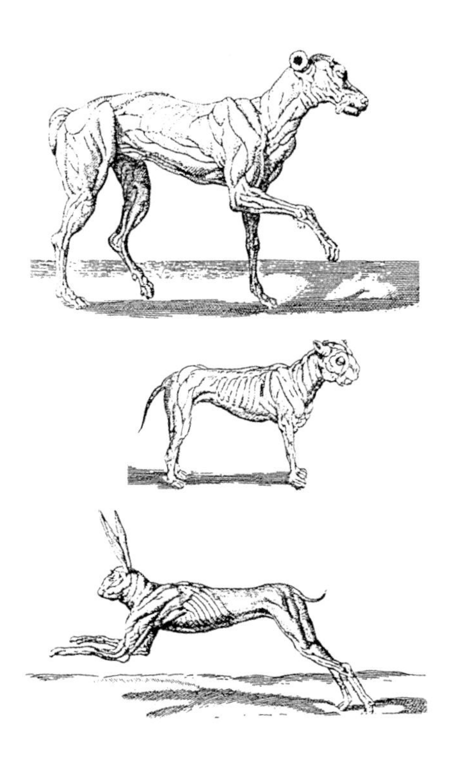

'Écorchés of a Dog, a Cat, and a Hare', by Crispijn van de Passe, 1643.

hares as illustrated in the natural histories. This fabulous animal seems to have been constructed, rather, in accordance with the perceived strangeness of all hares. Somewhere they just had to exist in this manifestly peculiar form, *contra naturam* and the observable evidence.

Some of the actual facts about hares, as currently recorded and understood, are perhaps no less remarkable than those mistakes, misprisions and exaggerations surveyed above. Plutarch thought there was something 'divine' about the speed of the hare; Thomas Pennant that 'to neglect pointing out the admirable contrivance of its several properties and parts, would be frustrating the chief design of this work: that of pointing out the divine wisdom in the animal world'.[32]

Divine wisdom aside, to watch a hare in full flight is indeed to get an idea of the physical limitations of the human body. It seems to be moving in a slightly different dimension, or to cover the ground without the usual constraints of gravity and lateral resistance. Like 'the shadow of a wind-driven cloud', or 'more like a low-flying bird than a running animal', according to one writer with a close lifelong knowledge of observing and poaching brown hares.[33] Even the word 'running' is not quite adequate to its bounding locomotion. Xenophon thought its body was so 'conformed' to function – specifically to rapid escape across open ground – that it could not walk. In fact Arctic hares do not touch the ground with their forelegs when at full tilt, and the exaggerated, immensely powerful hind legs of all hares (the first European account of a kangaroo likened it to a hare; Richard Jefferies thought the brown hare propelled itself 'almost like a grasshopper')[34] both enable their running speed and make ordinary walking what one writer has called 'almost a problem, almost a difficulty'.[35] The fastest hares can reach speeds as high as 45 miles per hour (72 km/h). When Lewis and Clark measured the leaps of the newly discovered white-tailed jackrabbit (a species of true hare, as are all American 'jackrabbits'), they found that it could cover the ground with leaps commonly between 18 and 22 feet, or 5.5 to 6.7 metres. Long thought to be virtually the most rapid thing on four legs, the brown hare is currently around seventh on the lists of the world's fastest land mammals, behind the cheetah, the American pronghorn and several types of gazelle. It can outstrip the greyhound – an animal six to ten times its size, and one which has been bred for centuries for its speed, owing its very existence in its present form to being matched against the hare.

It has also evolved other kinds of athleticism. A Greek fable has it that the hare evades the hound because one is running for its supper, the other for its life. Though the key advantage which it has over its man-made opponent is that it can make sharp, almost right-angled turns to escape. Greyhounds and hares can run at roughly 20 metres per second, but the hare's hind-limb hip-extensor and adductor muscles give it the edge.[36] Both kinds of muscle – the latter enabling rapid changes in direction, the former important for accelerating and jumping – are more exaggerated in the hare relative to the greyhound. On that notional island which Darwin described in his 1858 presentation to the Linnaean Society (the presentation in which he first used the idea of the struggle for existence as like 10,000 wedges being hammered together), an island on which greyhounds hunting both rabbits and hares might theoretically adapt, by getting faster, to hunt only hares if the rabbit population was to decline,[37] the dogs would need to work on their straight-running personal bests, but also to grow their hip-extensor and adductor muscles. Unlike the rabbit, whose principal line of defence is to make for its burrow, the hare fully justifies the cliché 'built for speed', with an athleticism seemingly out of all proportion to its size.

The hare currently belongs to an order, the Lagomorpha, from the Greek words for 'hare' and 'shape', which is one of the smallest in the animal kingdom. It contains just three genera (hares, rabbits and pikas), two families (Leporidae, the rabbits and hares, and Ochotonidae, the pikas) and fewer than 80 species, compared to some 1,685 species of rodent. If the hare has been and remains notoriously difficult to observe – as late as the 1970s it could be described by a specialist as 'the unknown animal',[38] and even the current specialist literature has frequent recourse to the proviso that 'not enough is currently known' about this

Skeleton of *Lepus capensis*, the most widespread African hare.

or that aspect of its behaviour – it has also proved difficult to categorize. Until recently anyone looking up the word 'hare' in the *Oxford English Dictionary* would find it referred to as a *rodent* quadruped (my emphasis), despite the fact that the article providing the basis for the removal of the lagomorphs from the order Rodentiae, largely on account of significant differences in dentition and cranial structure, was published nearly a century ago. Before 'becoming' rodents, hares were classified as ungulates by Linnaeus. Even the putative word of God erred in defining or placing them, for in Leviticus and Deuteronomy the hare is described as an animal that 'cheweth the cud' but 'divideth not the hoof' – a biblical way of saying that it was anomalous amongst ungulates, and therefore 'unclean'. In fact hares do not 'chew the cud', though they do digest their food twice, the second time in the form of soft excreted pellets. Zoologically speaking their status has both shifted and radically narrowed. What the lagomorphs have in common, and what distinguishes them as a separate order, is the possession of a second pair of upper incisors or 'peg teeth' behind their front pair and an elongated skull with lattice-like fenestrations or gaps in the cranial bone.

The lagomorphs make their appearance in the current fossil record some 55 million years ago; modern leporids in the late Miocene of Asia and Europe, 30 million years later. Considered to be among the oldest and most 'successful' of mammals, despite the fact that there are fewer than 30 extant species (only some of which were known to the early natural historians, who were mostly writing about *Lepus europaeus* and *Lepus timidus*), types of hare have adapted to exist in climates ranging from Arctic tundra to equatorial desert – finding a living from environments as different as cactus belt and alpine fell field; marsh and pampas – and extending from sea level to 5,500 metres above it in the Himalayas. The distribution of individual species varies from the vast to the tiny, with the European and Cape hares having two of the largest distributions of any mammal species. The Cape hare is found from West Africa to East China and as far south, as

'Northern Hare' or *Lepus americanus* in a winter pelage, from J. J. Audubon's *Viviparous Quadrupeds of North America*, 1854.

'Texan Hare' or *'Jackass Rabbit'*, from J. J. Audubon's *Viviparous Quadrupeds of North America*, 1854.

its name suggests, as the southernmost tip of South Africa. The Arctic hare is circumpolar and reaches 83 degrees north on Ellesmere Island. The snowshoe hare extends from Alaska to Newfoundland, penetrating as far south as northern New Mexico, while the distribution of the brown or European hare includes South America, Australia, New Zealand and elsewhere due to successful importation dating from the mid-nineteenth century. The mountain hare extends from Ireland's Atlantic coast to the east coast of the Pacific. The black-tailed jackrabbit extends from Washington and South Dakota to Baja California, and from the Pacific coast almost to the Mississippi. On the other hand the broom hare is found only in northern Spain's Cantabrian mountains; the black jackrabbit exists only on Espiritu Island in the Gulf of California; the Ethiopian highland hare is restricted to the central plain of Shoa province, and the Tehunatepec jackrabbit is confined to some 150 square km of Oaxaca and Chiapas. Numbers of this last-named type are shrinking and the species is endangered. But the number of hare species is hardly immutable for another reason. It ranges from a dozen to around 30 depending on the classification used, and it is always possible that new classifications will be made, with sub-species reclassified as species and vice versa.[39]

When Bewick wrote of his chimerical 'harvesting hare', he must have been referring unwittingly to the hay-piling behaviour of alpine pikas. Pikas are small, short-eared and rodent-like, bearing no outward physical resemblance to the leporids. They are not, as their inclusion in the order might suggest, 'hare-shaped'. The vernacular naming of hare species is also potentially confusing, for with the exception of the Arctic hare and snowshoe hare, the American hares are called 'jackrabbits' – a fact which is explained by early European settlers' likening of their elongated ears to those of the jackass. Mark Twain, on seeing his first 'jackass rabbit' may have thought it was 'well named', since it 'has the most preposterous ears that ever were mounted on any creature but a jackass',[40] but the inclusion of 'rabbit' in that name has contributed to popular tendencies to conflate or confuse leporids. Most of the salient characteristics of hares can in fact be usefully presented in the way they differ from rabbits.

Hares are generally much larger: longer and leggier, giving an impression of stature enhanced by their generally much longer ears. They reach weights of 5 kg in the far north, averaging 3 in temperate zones (with some exceptions) and 2 at the equator, frequently occupying a unique position as the only animals of their weight in a given environment. The brown hare is about the size of a domestic cat. Rabbits are gregarious with relatively complex family groups; hares mostly solitary with minimal pair bonding among promiscuous adults and relatively little parental care of their young. The relatively complex coat colour of hares, including seasonal changes, is linked to their reliance upon

Relative sizes of brown hare, mountain hare (*Lepus timidus*) and rabbit (*Oryctolagus cuniculus*).

camouflage as well as speed. Their speed, camouflage, lack of family life and even size are linked as adaptations to their principal behavioural difference from the rabbit, namely, the fact that they do not burrow. Though there are exceptions to this rule, with certain desert-dwelling hares using or extending the burrows of other animals to escape the sun, and with mountain hares occasionally using short burrows to escape predation from above, most hares make do instead with a 'form' or resting place which consists of only a narrow scrape on the surface of the earth. As a result of this, or in intimate parallel connection to being 'unhoused' or unprotected, hares are extremely precocial. For whereas rabbits, like most small mammals, are born blind and naked in a prepared 'nest', leverets are born fully furred, able to see, and able to move about soon after birth. Or 'with their clothes on, with full sight and ready to go',[41] as one countryman has it. Whereas the rabbit is a large small animal, the hare has developed in ways more consistent with being a small large one. In addition to outward and visible differences, hares have also diverged anatomically from other leporids in order to avoid predation. Their athleticism is further enabled by a relatively lighter skeleton, and actually lighter skull and by the fact that they have relatively larger hearts and lungs and a relatively large amount of blood and a wider nasal passage. The brown hare's heart weighs from 1 to 1.8 per cent of its total body weight, compared to 0.3 per cent in rabbits. The voluntary muscles of brown hares are adapted to high endurance requirements, with more capillaries per square millimetre, more myoglobin and more oxidative voluntary muscle fibres allowing higher oxidative capacity.

Hares have also developed relatively complex escape and concealment strategies in addition to speed, endurance and camouflage. They can swim, even on occasion into the sea when hard pressed. The brown hare in particular employs elaborate means to confuse its scent trail, including doubling back on its

Newborn, furred Arctic hares (*Lepus arcticus*).

Newborn, furless Eastern cottontail rabbits (*Sylvilagus floridanus*).

Black-tailed jackrabbit, Joshua Tree National Park, California.

tracks; leaping sideways to break the trail; entering and leaving its form in ways designed to construct a 'maze' for predators hunting by scent. They also establish regular routes or 'race-tracks' in the vicinity of their forms, and 'meuses' or gaps in hedges and fences facilitating rapid egress from enclosed fields. And if their sheer speed across open ground enabled the development of hare 'coursing' with greyhounds, it was the full range of the brown hare's abilities to evade and bewilder its pursuers that gave the hare virtually pre-eminent standing in *par force* hunting with packs of scent-hounds.

Their senses are also acute. Thomas Pennant may have quaintly compared hares' ears to 'the tubes made use of by the deaf',[42] but their long, mobile ears are adapted to acute hearing as well as to the regulation of body temperature (the desert-dwelling antelope jackrabbit has the longest ears of any hare) and, contrary to the beliefs of the early naturalists, they also have good eyesight, with eyes so positioned in the skull to afford exceptional peripheral vision. Perceptions of their poor eyesight probably had to do with the fact they will rely on camouflage and immobility before speed, not bolting at the first sign of danger but sometimes sitting tight in their forms until the last moment. In *The Voyage of the 'Beagle'* Darwin describes an Indian method of catching the varying hare by walking slowly up to it in a narrowing spiral,[43] and there are recent anecdotal accounts of taking the brown hare during daylight in a similar way. As for the notion that they slept 'with open eyes' – the notion that has given us the word 'lagopthalmia' to describe a medical condition in which the eyelids are severely contracted, and which the Jungian psychoanalyst John Layard thought actually referred to the animal's symbolic association with spiritual intuition or vigilance rather than to fact – George Ewart Evans and David Thomson could find as late as 1971 'no conclusive evidence' for or against it, when researching their book *The Leaping Hare*.[44] It's now thought that

Antelope jackrabbit.

hares do achieve full sleep, with eyes closed, but for remarkably short periods of time hardly exceeding several minutes' duration.

Despite their reputation for rapid increase and hyper-sexuality, hares are not especially prolific breeders compared to rabbits – much less so compared to rodents. Their litters range from just one, of six to eight leverets, in the extreme north, to eight litters of one or two young at the equator, giving a constant annual figure of around ten, compared with up to 45 in rabbits. But the brown hare does exhibit one extraordinary reproductive capacity which has provided, in the exaggerated descriptions given of it from Aristotle onwards, the basis for its reputation for unique and almost preternatural sexual proclivities and increase. Unlike most mammals, both female rabbits and hares will continue

A brown hare, south-east Australia.

to mate while pregnant. But only the brown hare is capable of conceiving a second time – of carrying two potential litters at different stages of development. Superfetation, as it is called, can occur as a rare event in most mammals, even in humans. It has been recorded in populations of brown hares in up to 13 per cent of females, a remarkably high and probably conservative figure. For Aristotle it was a primary characteristic of hares – and subsequent writers almost competed with each other to emphasize and exaggerate its miraculousness. For Herodotus, in a passage that was to be echoed even by eighteenth-century natural historians reflecting on the relative fertility of predator and prey species, and by William Paley on the balance between predation and super-fecundity, it was:

European brown hares, male and female, during courtship.

> Hard not to believe that divine providence, in the wisdom that one would expect of it, has made prolific every kind of creature which is timid and preyed upon by others, in order to ensure its continuance, while savage and noxious species are comparatively unproductive. Hares, for instance, which are the prey to all sorts of animals, not to mention birds and men, are excessively prolific; they are the only animals in which superfetation occurs, and you will find in a hare's womb young in all stages of development, some with fur on, others with none, others just beginning to form, and others, again, barely conceived.[45]

For Oppian the emphasis upon its extraordinary powers of increase was matched by another, also typical, upon the 'unceasing' sexual drive of both male and female hares which must enable it: 'Unceasingly they yearn to mate and while the females are still pregnant they do not reject the lustful advances of the male, not even when they carry in their wombs the swift arrow of fruitfulness. For this tribe, among all that the infinite earth breeds, is the most prolific.'[46]

It was upon such accounts, I would argue, with their wild exaggeration upon a still remarkable modicum of truth, that the widespread and various uses of the hare in symbolic sexual contexts were established. Though simple observation of the mating behaviour of hares, with its headlong and sometimes violent sexual chases; 'boxing' between males and females as well as between males, and multiple, promiscuous and rapid copulations (the male brown hare has been observed to copulate seven times with different partners in the space of two and a half hours) – the behaviour which also accounts for its reputed 'madness' in March – would perhaps have provided grounds enough for their sexual symbolization, if not for its range. It is currently thought that superfetation in hares is enabled by the fact that sperm can survive in females for up to 40 days. As a means of effectively shortening gestation, it contributes to their ability to produce a rapid succession of litters. For Plutarch and readers of his Renaissance translators, the superfetating hare provided an emblem for usury and the rapid 'reproduction' of debt; for the poet Apollinaire an analogy for the fertility of the poetic mind. More in the mainstream, as presented in the classical near-miraculous accounts of it, the hare's capacity to superfetate must have also contributed to general perceptions of its uniqueness and mystery.

Due to their relatively exposed way of living hares have an unusually high number of predators, with high mortality rates among their young. Adult hares live on average no more than one year, compared to a potential lifespan of up to twelve years. There is an epigram by Ausonius in which a hare hunted to the seashore by dogs and men cries out, before being eaten by a dog-fish, that 'all rape of land and sea is on me/ even of the heavens, if there is a dog-star'. An ironic conclusion, since in the southern night sky there is both a 'dog-star' and a 'lepus' constellation at the foot of the hunter Orion. If due to its number of predators and exposure to predation the hare has been symbolically utilized as a quintessential prey species or analogue for 'victimhood', an increased understanding of the impact upon certain of their species by intensive agriculture has hardly diminished their status as such. Changes in agricultural practices have meant that hares, and especially leverets, have had to contend with additional mortalities from grass-cutting, the burning of stubble, the use of herbicides, fungicides and insecticides, as well as from road deaths. Organophosphates do not cause death but will reduce activity and capacity for survival. The increased use of cereal crops without rotation, cleared in

September, leaves the hare in certain cases with nothing but bare earth from one horizon to another until November. The number of brown hares in certain parts of Europe has greatly declined, in Britain by some three quarters in the past century.

Marooned off the coast of South America, Robinson Crusoe finds himself protecting his nascent crops against unruly hares as well as birds; Buffon includes the hare in a chapter beginning with a reflection on the propensity of certain animals to multiply uncontrollably. Even the risible 1970s horror movie, *Night of the Lepus*, resurrects fears of the timid jackrabbit becoming a nightmarish foe, albeit in the form of giant animals modified in the usual scientific experiment gone wrong. But unlike rabbits with their well-known propensity to multiply to extreme pest and even plague proportions, and with the notable exception of the snowshoe hare, the only exclusively boreal species, which experiences regular population rises and crashes (part of the so-called 'lynx–hare cycle' which has provided both an important model for predator–prey interaction and an analogy or homology for the behaviour of economic markets), hares generally regulate their population density at levels far below the carrying capacity of a given environment. Though the brown hare has been a significant agricultural pest when translocated (as in parts of North America in the nineteenth century), or when protected for sport, William Cobbett was surely exaggerating when in *Rural Rides* he reported seeing 'an acre of hares'[47] – an exaggeration underwritten by his opposition to game laws which prevented even tenant farmers, let alone the rural populace, from killing them. The apparent self-regulation of their numbers by hare populations in general has led to at least the speculation that their social behaviour must be more complex than previously thought – though 'speculation' is very much the operative word. It remains a curious fact that hares have been

A lynx chasing a snowshoe hare.

relatively little studied, with even their primary characteristics and behaviours remaining open to much further inquiry.

Hares have been utilized in ways which reflect their behaviour and physical characteristics. Though individual hares can be tamed, the fact that they do not thrive or breed well in captivity has been a factor in the divergence of their utility value from that of rabbits. As well as in their cultural availability as a cipher for headlong wildness, with even one of the few modern monographs on hares entitled, tautologically or with zoological redundancy, *Wild Hares*.[48] The domestication of rabbits in medieval Europe enabled both the farming of them for food and their subsequent widespread current use in medical and other experiments; the elusiveness of hares enabled their central importance in the theory and practice of hunting with hounds, and in European game law and in anti-hunting discourses. And though hares have been hunted for thousands of years for both food and fur, including in the modern period on a massive scale (it is estimated that in pre-Revolutionary Russia some six million skins of hares were sold annually), the character of their flesh and pelts has determined and refined usage. European hare fur was not suitable for use by furriers, due to the relative weakness of attachment between skin and fur on hare pelts. It was used as trimming on garments, but most valued for its felting properties. High-quality felt can be produced from hare pelts, which fetched a good price well into the nineteenth century when sold for that purpose, providing a staple material for the hatters' trade. Beaten industrial felt was also used in papermaking machines, as well as for insulating and polishing, finding its way into homes in the marginal form of dampers on piano keys and baize on billiard tables. An ersatz 'luxury' use for its fur was devised in the fur industry through the production, after a process of shaving and dyeing, of 'Electric Seal'.[49]

Ingenious non-industrial usages of hare fur include that devised by the Hareskin Indians of Canada's Northwest Territories – a method of cutting it into spiral strips that were then sewn together to make traditional garments. In addition to the value of hare *materia* for medical usage, throughout the medieval period the skin of the animal was also to be found between the covers of books. For while vellum was produced exclusively from the hides of cows, parchment was made from the skin of a variety of animals, including that of hares – so that a medieval manuscript with a marginal depiction of a hare might actually have been written upon the animal's skin, and even 'illuminated' with brushes made from its fur, brushes which were traditionally used by goldsmiths. Other curious marginal uses range from the nineteenth-century practice of carrying a piece of hare fur as a kind of flea-magnet, to the current use of 'hare masks' (skin and fur pulled from dead hares' heads like gloves,with the ears and vibrissae attached) as source-material to make flies for fly-fishing. In the 1960s the US military stockpiled cultures of the disease tularemia for potential use as a biological weapon: a weapon which may thus have partly derived from hares, since tularemia is common among both hares and rabbits.

As for their use as food, hares have been eaten in most parts of the world, in contexts ranging from those in which hare flesh was as an important staple, to others in which its meat was constructed as a luxury item. In the Kama–Volga region in the the 1960s it was estimated that the meat from all hares caught weighed as much as 50,000 cows, providing more than half of the animal protein eaten. Huge numbers of hare are still shot annually throughout Europe and North America, though there are no figures detailing how many of these are killed purely for sport. Historically speaking, and when not determined by sheer necessity, the status of hares as food has been affected not just by the European game laws designed to restrict their consumption, but by reactions to their dark meat – which range from extreme delectation to equally extreme distaste or even taboo – and to a lesser degree by dietary theory. The Galenic notion that to eat a hare was potentially deleterious was given extreme expression by Tobias Venner, for whom the hare 'breedeth melancholy more than any other flesh',[50] though one seventeenth-century writer sceptically qualified his reporting of the belief with the fact that 'there are jolly huntsmen who eat it every day'.[51] The poet Martial (*c.* AD 41–104) thought that the hare was the most delicious of all quadrupeds, exaggerating but still reflecting wider Roman and later refined European taste; the first recipe book in English includes three elaborate 'receits' for cooking hares. That superlatives regarding hare flesh, and knowledge of its preparation, were not confined to gastronomical exquisites or to that tradition of exclusive gastronomy initiated by *The Forme of Cury* (*c.* 1390) is best exemplified by a comment in John James Audubon's *Quadrupeds of America*, in which a 'dish of hares' provided for its author by native Americans is said to be one of the best meals he'd ever tasted.[52]

Hare 'masks' as sold for use in fly-fishing.

Postcard showing jokily outsized 'West Texas Jackrabbit' being gutted.

In *The Physiology of Taste* (1825), however, Jean-Anthelme Brillat-Savarin reflects the high status of the hare as game in the nineteenth century, and takes to its limit a connoisseurial distinction designed to both demonstrate his own exquisiteness and refine the animal's status as 'luxury' food. For Brillat-Savarin the leveret 'is perhaps the most savoury of all quadrupeds', but not just any leveret. It needs to be one of a certain age, and 'born in the parched highlands of Valromey or Upper Dauphine.'[53]

In England the rather less exquisite but still socially narrow taste for 'jugged hare', a dish made with stock traditionally thickened with the animal's own blood – and redolent of country houses, parsonages, academic and military high tables –

survived into the era of Mrs Beeton and beyond, whereas Hannah Glasse's recipe for spit-roasted hare reflected its eighteenth-century incorporation into aspirant and middle-class cuisine. Beeton suggests the use of port rather than blood when 'jugging'– a concession to squeamishness, perhaps, with the port adding a further 'classy' element – though the illustration to her recipe for roast hare shows the animal with its head still on,[54] contrary to a change in taste or sensibility which William Hazlitt had articulated with specific regard to leporids: 'Animals that are made use of as food should either be so small as to be imperceptible, or else we should . . . not leave the form standing to reproach us with our gluttony and cruelty. I hate to see a rabbit trussed, or a hare brought to the table in the form which it occupied while living.'[55]

In the 1890s a writer on hare cuisine suggested the use of a symbol on menus to disguise for the squeamish the presence of hares' blood; a recent writer has described jugged hare served at an Oxford college as 'the animal paraded in its most debased form',[56] and while it is necessary to imagine, when considering its construction as 'luxury' food, what a medieval peasant or nineteenth century agricultural worker might have made of refined reactions to hare meat (let alone a Canadian trapper, North American Indian or African tribesman), there is an equal and opposite tradition of repugnance towards both hare flesh and the very idea of eating it. For it is 'surtout abominable' according to one eighteenth-century culinary authority in the mainstream of this parallel tradition;[57] unpalatable even to certain of those who have hunted and 'poached' it – and tabooed in orthodox Judaism and in Islam. Other taboos on eating hare flesh include those of the pagan Britons and of the Namaqua Indians, the latter explained by Frazer as due to fear that it will cause those eating it to become as 'cowardly' as the animal itself:

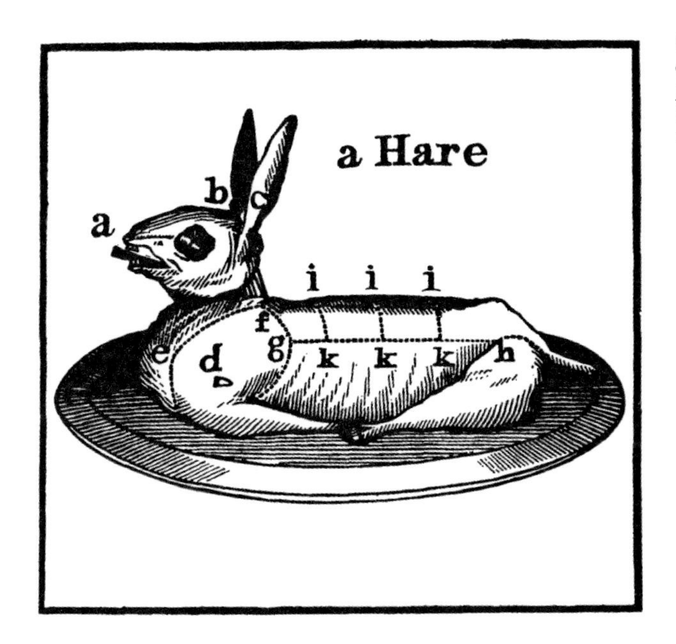

Butcher's diagram of a hare, from John Trusler's *The Honours of the Table*, 1788.

a warlike version of the Roman conceit that consuming its flesh would make one as sexually potent as a hare.[58]

If the hare has punched somewhat above its weight in world mythology, it has also provided writers and artists with an unusually flexible symbolic device. There is a letter by the poet Ted Hughes in which he describes a hare, in symbolic relation to the protagonist of a work in progress: 'the hare is the tiger is the women is his blood is all kinds of things. I'm not quite sure.'[59] Due to its historical multivalence, the archive of associations which it has generated, the hare is ripe to be thus squeezed for maximum, even ultimately uncertain or inchoate significance. Amongst the kinds of things which it has been made or co-opted to signify is, precisely, this poetically open-ended or resonant quality. That said, they tend to cluster around a number of areas more or less troped upon its natural history: sex, death, speed and vitality; super-sensitivity, elusiveness and cunning; untamed or unfathomable 'wildness', with only their sinister portentousness bucking the trend.

Sexual uses extend from painted vases of the fifth century BC depicting the Greek practice of giving live hares as love-gifts, to the use of the animal as one of the three male body-types in the *Kama Sutra*; from such witty metaphor as that used by the Provençal poet Arnaut Daniel, when likening himself to a hare-hunter 'on ox-back' (a figure for his pursuit of an unattainable woman),[60] to Shakespearean bawdy, with the word 'bawdy' itself possibly linked to an old English name for a hare, 'bawd'. In the folk ballad 'The Bonnie Black Hare' the animal becomes explicitly linked to what a peasant woman has 'under her skirts'.[61] And if the association between hares and female genitalia was traditional, priapic associations run from Chaucer's hare-hunting and 'lusting' Monk, to the moment in David Lynch's film *Wild at Heart* (1990), in which a character threatens to belabour another 'like a big old jackrabbit', in a scene which blurs the boundary of seduction and rape. Even Vladimir Nabokov, no friend to symbolism, animal or otherwise, had occasion to point out to an interviewer (for *Playboy* magazine, with its notorious 'bunny' logo) that he had given the heroine of his sexually scandalous *Lolita* a surname, Haze, 'where Irish mists blend with a German bunny – I mean, a small German hare'.[62] With this pun upon the German word for 'hare', *Hase,* the novelist was hardly endorsing the conversion of the teenaged Dolores Haze to sexual use or cipher, but subverting the tradition, partly by activating another of the animal's traditional roles as defenceless and 'innocent' victim. Such double-think is present in earnest in *Shot-down Hare* by Anna Fasshauer, a photo of a dead hare placed on the blood-smeared floor of a Dutch brothel.[63]

When W. B. Yeats wrote of staring through a hare-bone in his poem 'The Collar-Bone of a Hare', and of laughing 'at all those who marry in churches', he was tapping into the animal's reputation for unlicensed sexuality, and for attractively irreducible 'wildness'.[64] There is a moment in D. H. Lawrence's *Women in Love* in which the character Birkin looks forward to a world cleared of a 'dirty' humanity. 'Don't you find it a beautiful clean thought', Birkin asks Ursula, 'a world empty of people, just uninterrupted grass, and a hare sitting up?'[65] Birkin's sentiment is nothing if not eccentric, even pathological. And yet the animal with which he chooses to illustrate it is aptly chosen, for its traditional reputation for peculiar independence and freedom, as a cipher for unsullied natural wildness and vitality. You only have to substitute 'rabbit', let alone 'rat' or 'fox' to see how this works. Its use here as the totem animal of a post-apocalyptic future also depends upon its availability to represent a 'deep' past, as part of Birkin's, and Lawrence's, critique of industrialism. A more recent, naturalistic and extended variation of the theme of the 'anarchic' hare running beyond the pale of the human society which it has liminally haunted, is present in Arto Paasilinna's novel *The Year of the Hare*. A wounded hare picked up on a remote Finnish road provides its protagonist with an epiphany causing him to go AWOL from a loveless marriage and stale journalistic career. And to take with him on the aimless road trip which ensues, on his line of flight, both the actual animal and emblem of his revolt from 'bourgeois' conformity and late twentieth-century consumerism.

The hare's fleetness and vitality have been taken in various symbolic directions, including as reminders of the fleetingness of existence: from still-life paintings to Sam Taylor-Wood's video 'A Little Death', a speeded-up film of a decaying hare. In the Polish poet Czesław Miłosz's 'Encounter' a glimpsed hare functions rather like the sparrow in the Venerable Bede's famous comparison of life itself to a bird flying through a banqueting hall.[66] In Wallace Stevens's 'The Jack-Rabbit', the hare's joyful 'carolling' is linked to the image of a buzzard on a winding-sheet, and to the 'rattling entrails' of an actual raptor lying in pre-determined wait for the hare.[67] As for 'sinister' hares, two final examples show their survival into the late twentieth century and how their symbolic resonance has been available to popular as well as to high culture. When the exhumed coffin of a child is opened as part of a murder investigation in the film *The Wicker Man* (1973) it is found to contain not a human corpse but a hare. In a more

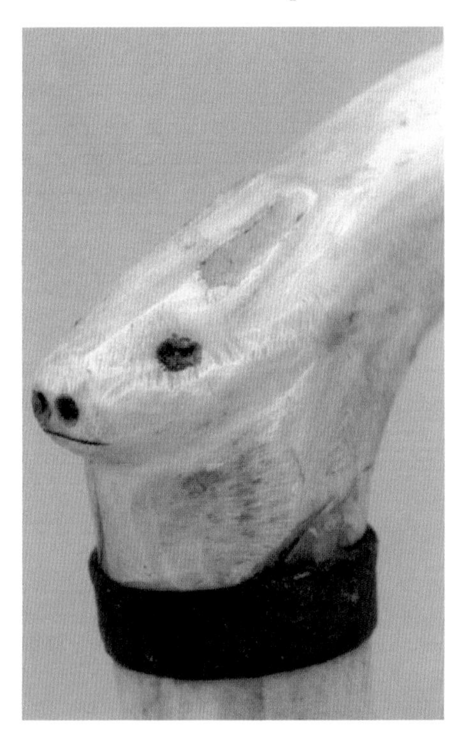

Inuit carving of an Arctic hare head, on a cane made from a narwhal's tusk.

recent film, *Donnie Darko* (2001), an anthropomorphized jackrabbit features as a kind of sinister alter ego of its teenaged main character: a symptom of incipient psychosis, but also the vehicle of his exposure of the sexual misdemeanours of a local lifestyle guru and lecturer to high schools on clean living and moral uplift.

When George Ewart Evans and David Thomson were collecting hare lore from interviewees in the 1970s they added to the taboos on hare flesh mentioned above the belief, still surviving at that time in County Leitrim, Ireland, that their sinister associations complicated their suitability, or desirability, as food. Or as one countryman put it: 'people wouldn't eat a hare. They say they are bewitched or that there is something uncanny about them. *They are not right*.'[68] Such reactions lead us away from considerations of natural history, material utility and literary symbolism – back into the regions of myth, folklore and religion.

2 Mythic Hare

When a hare crosses the path of the eponymous anti-hero in Miguel de Cervantes' *Don Quixote*, he is moved to anxiously exclaim '*malum signum, malum signum*', if only before a less superstitious Sancho Panza steps in to reassure him.[1] The ominous nature of the hare, its role as a 'bad sign', is testified to by numerous survivals in folklore of beliefs concerning its negative significance. Among the names heaped upon it in 'The Names of the Hare', a medieval poem couched in the form of a charm designed to divest it of its power, are 'the one who makes you shudder' and 'the one who makes you flee', as well as 'the creature that none dare name'.[2] In parts of Britain even into the twentieth century it was considered by fishermen bad luck to utter the word 'hare' at sea, whilst a hare seen running through a village street presaged an outbreak of house-fires.[3] According to the memoirs of a Napoleonic general, the Emperor fell from his horse while reconnoitring the banks of the Niemen on the eve of the ill-fated invasion of Russia when his mount was startled by a running hare. A sure sign, as one of those present interpreted it, that the invasion should not take place.[4]

The earliest recorded instance of an omen involving hares depends not upon the ominous nature of the animal itself, but upon a complex literary utilization of its place in a wider mythic fabric. In his *Oresteia* (*c*. 458 BC), a trilogy of plays beginning with the return of the Greeks from Troy, Aeschylus included in its first scene a flashback to their departure in which the chorus tells of how two eagles, one black, one white, were seen feeding on a hare 'richly pregnant with young that had missed the last laps of its race'.[5] This is interpreted in the play as auspicious, with the eagles signifying Agamemnon and Menelaus 'feeding on' a defeated and captured Troy. But crucially the goddess Artemis, who was antagonistic to the expedition, is angry with the eagles (birds that are messengers of or symbols of Zeus) for killing the hare, in her capacity as 'protectress of all sucking animals'. In this way the image is made to actually presage or foreshadow the eventual downfall of Agamemnon and Menelaus. The image as well as the hare is pregnant with its own nemesis, with the fall of the house of Atreus as well as with the destruction of Troy.

One of the earliest appearances of the hare in world literature, in Homer's *Iliad,* similarly depends upon its emblematic association with the eagle, in a scene which relates the combat between Hector and Achilles. It owes its presence there to its suitability to extended comparisons between warfare and hunting, and between warfare and predator/prey relationships –

Sicilian coin depicting golden eagles feeding on a hare, c. 411 BC.

and specifically to the fact that one of its traditional predators was the bird of Zeus, or of 'Jove', in Pope's translation, in which Hector begins the fight thus:

> Fierce, at the word, his weighty sword he drew,
> And, all collected, on Achilles flew.
> So Jove's bold bird, high balanced in the air,
> Stoops from the clouds to truss the quivering hare.[6]

It is Achilles, though, who eventually prevails. And in doing so Homer shows him reversing the terms of this comparison as well as Hector's initial advantage. Achilles bores two holes through the ankles of Hector's corpse and ties it to his chariot with a thong threaded between them. Trusses him, in other words, like a hare, and then mutilates the body by dragging it behind the chariot. It's a particularly ignoble end for a warrior who elsewhere in the poem has been compared to a lion, and it is accompanied by the jeering of the Greeks. This sequence of images was to prove suggestive in the European emblematic tradition, in images of hares approaching or biting the dead body of a lion. One such image is accompanied by a text linking it explicitly to the death of Hector: 'The Greekes most gladde, his dying corpse assaile,/ Who late did flee before him in the fielde'.[7] The hare/lion emblem also had behind it the Latin proverb 'even hares can insult a dead lion'. Both tended to be used for politically conservative purposes, ranging from illustration of 'unnatural' challenges to regal authority, to the liberties taken by subjects 'in the absence of their governour'.[8] These emblematic and proverbial off-shoots only serve to show the relative complexity of Homer's extended lion/eagle/hare motif. It acts as a figure for the extremity of Hector's fall (from top predator to proverbially 'timorous' prey species); for the sudden and total

Roman mural painting with hanging hare and mask of satyr, *c.* 40–30 BC.

reversal of fortune in battle (Hector and Achilles contending, so to speak, as to who should 'be' the hare; with Achilles winning the war of metaphors); and for the uncertain role of divine providence. Since the eagle is the bird of Zeus, both parties assume that they have the gods on their side. But by treating the body of Hector as so much dead meat, Achilles (now the eagle) oversteps the mark delimiting how far it's acceptable to be 'like a beast' and retain the approval of the gods. There is likely to be another reversal of fortune in train.

Look up 'hare' in a work such as Hans Biedermann's *Dictionary of Symbolism* and you will find it described as 'not distinguished from rabbits, either in symbolism or popular superstition.'[9] Despite some mythic overlap between leporids, especially with regard to lunar symbolism, it's a statement which hardly makes sense. Not least because the Greeks, the originators in Europe of a complex symbolic and mythic role for the hare, had no such role for the rabbit, an animal which was only introduced there in the first century BC. A Greek word for rabbit, 'half-hare', is derived from its difference in size but also reflects

A Levantine, probably Syrian, gypsum vessel in the form of a hare, c. 6,400–5,900 BC.

Egyptian jade amulet in the form of a seated hare with anthropomorphic face, c. 600–300 BC. Believed to confer speed or fertility on its wearer, or resurrection after death.

its conceptually and historically subordinate character. And contrary to Biedermann, a whole work could be written on the animal's specific appearances in world myth and folklore alone.

The hare probably makes its first appearance in a mythic or religious context in association with the Hittite god, Rundas. As does the motif of the hare in the talons of an eagle, an emblem for martial 'victory' or imperial power that was to have a long afterlife in Europe, including in Rome, and in Nazi Germany where the hare was replaced by a swastika. But it was with the Egyptians that a fully fledged symbolic role for the animal first originated, though much of the evidence for it is slippery and subject to conjecture. It may seem attractively appropriate, for instance, that the hieroglyph meaning 'to be' – a long-eared hare above a stylized wave – is derived from the actual creature's quickness and vitality. But nowhere in the hieroglyphs does the figure of a hare actually mean 'hare'. It is, rather, a phonetic symbol. That said, a recent work offers an example of a hieroglyph which appears to include the idea of the animal rather than simply its phonetic value: a hare plus human legs meaning 'to hurry up', along with others more cryptic: with sparrow meaning 'fault, blame'; with hair or branches meaning 'stripped off'/ 'hairless'. And of key importance in the language: with sun disk and rays of light meaning 'light'; with door-leaf meaning 'to open'.[10]

As for the association of the creature with Egyptian gods and goddesses, there is a depiction of a hare-headed divinity called 'Unnut' at the temple of Dendera in Egypt. This mistress of the city is mentioned in the *Book of the Dead*, which also provides an indication of her great antiquity, even by Egyptian standards. With the body of a woman and head of a hare, she is depicted holding a sceptre in one hand and the glyph for 'life' in the other. Evidence suggests that in remote antiquity there was a temple in her honour at Hermopolis, and that she was the old local goddess of the nome (an administrative division of Ancient Egypt). According to E. Wallis Budge,

> The standards which represent the nomes of Egypt are distinguished by figures of birds and animals, e.g., the hawk, the bull, the hare, etc., But it is not clear whether these are intended to represent 'totems' or not . . . the animal or bird standing at the top of the nome-perch or standard is not intended for a fetish or a representation of a tribal ancestor, but for a creature which was regarded as the deity under whose protection the people of a

Tomb painting showing hares being carried in as food for the dead.

ΜΕΣΣΑΝΙΩΝ
MESSE
ΜΕΣΣΑΝΙΩΝ

> certain tract of territory was placed, and we may assume that within the limits of that territory it was unlawful to injure or kill such animal or bird.[11]

This latter observation represents the earliest instance of a sacred taboo on eating hare flesh. There was also in ancient Egypt a hare-headed god, depicted for instance in a vignette in which he sits with a snake-headed god and a bull-headed god. In company, that is, with animals of great sacred significance. A hare-headed god also guards one of the Seven Halls in the underworld. Attempts have also been made to link the hare with the most important of all Egyptian gods. At Dendera a hare-headed god, wrapped in mummy swathing, is seen with hands in such a position as to suggest his identification with Osiris. According to the French Egyptologist E. LePage Renouf, one of the names of Osiris, 'Un-nefer', is to be interpreted as meaning 'Glorious Hare'. Osiris 'sprang up' like the hare, which, as the rising sun, is said to be the 'springer'. He also argued for the connection between the moon and the hare, and the subsidiary aspect of Osiris as a moon-deity, though it should be noted that other Egyptologists have disputed his reading, on involved linguistic grounds beyond the ken of non-specialists.[12]

Images of hares can be found on a wide range of Greek artefacts: on amphorae, bowls, dishes and bronze vessels; on wedding and other rings; necklaces, mirror surrounds, in mural paintings; in the form of zoomorphic scent bottles, and on coins. The motif of eagles, or a single eagle, feeding on or carrying off a hare appears on numerous Greek coins. But it also takes its place there with many other designs including hares. On Sicilian coins of the fifth century BC there are single, gracefully designed leaping hares; a hare leaping over a dolphin above a wave; a hare over a grasshopper, and another leaping over a fly; a hare over an ear of corn,

Hare motifs on Sicilian coins, 5th century BC.

Nike above; a hare springing over a scallop shell; and another with Pan sitting on a rock. There is also a hare with a dolphin below and a cock above it; a hare springing between a shell and a hippocampus; and a hound standing, head averted, with an inverted hare below. Though the last of these is merely naturalistic, a hunting scene, and though some of the others clearly allude to naturalistic attributes of the creature (chiefly its speed and athleticism, relating it to the dolphin, grasshopper and fly as well as to Nike) the presence of the ear of corn also signifies its symbolic association with fertility and increase, just as the presence of Pan alerts us to the association of the hare with the gods and goddesses of the wild and of the chase.

Artemis pities the pregnant hare in *Agamemnon* in her capacity as goddess of the hunt, of wild animals and of childbirth. According to Xenophon it was good hunting practice to begin a hunt with a prayer to the goddess and, according to the Greco-Roman historian and philosopher Arrian, leverets should be spared in her honour. The Greeks also associated the hare with Aphrodite and Eros, and with the Bacchic mythical and ritual cycle. Philostratus describes the hare as 'the most acceptable sacrifice' to Aphrodite (the Greek Venus) on account of 'the legend of the hare, that it possesses the gift of Aphrodite (fertility) to a superlative degree'.[13] On vases and other artefacts we can find images of a satyr trying to catch a hare; six satyrs armed with clubs chasing one; a satyr playing with a hare, holding out to it a string of beads; a hare in a cave attending a meeting between Dionysus, a satyr and a maenad; a satyr seen teasing a panther by holding out a hare, while another offers one to the young Dionysus; two satyrs watching a pair of hares playing together; a bearded Dionysus receiving a hare from two maenads, and so on. The Erotes, and Eros himself, are frequently depicted running or flying in pursuit of a hare, or flying off with a live one, or running after one with dogs. Artefacts are also extant which show Erotes watching hares playing; drawing a chariot pulled by hares; playing with and even kissing a hare; and rushing upon a hare emerging from a snail-shell. Images of Hermaphroditus chasing hares probably derive from the notion that hares could change their gender, or be both male and female at once. The promiscuous Aphrodite was the mother of Hermaphroditus, fathered by Dionysus, as well as of Priapus, and her adulteries included a relationship with Ares, the god of war. This mythic fabric links fertility, hunting, war, hermaphroditism and unlicensed or hyper-sexuality, making the hare, an animal associated with all of these elements, a creature of peculiarly multivalent if not to say overdetermined symbolic potential.

The use of the hare as a sexual symbol or emblem was not unique to Greece. But there are vase-paintings depicting a practice that was: the giving of live hares as love-gifts. Examples of those images include men offering hares to women, usually in a lightly eroticized scenario. And men offering the creatures to other men, usually an older man making the gift to a younger, depicted in such a way as to make the sexual meaning of the image explicit. In one such image the hare is stretched out horizontally to make a physical connection between the standing figure who holds it by its back legs and ears, and the seated youth on whose shoulders the front legs of the hare rest. This stretching out of the hare, and the artist's skill in painting it, gives to its body a lithe or nubile character which enhances and further clarifies its homoeroticism. Use of the hare in Greek sexual symbolism in general ranges from its role in proximity to the 'lasciviousness' of the satyrs, to the playful eroticism of the erotes or cupids; from the dark sexual energies of Dionysus to the fruitfulness of Aphrodite and the chastity of Artemis, and from contexts in which there is a rape implied to the graceful homoeroticism of genre scenes. It is here, too, that we find the origin of the idea that if hunting was like war, it was also like sexual pursuit. In Xenophon's memoir of Socrates there is a passage specifically comparing in great detail a hare hunt with the 'pursuit' of a lover.[14]

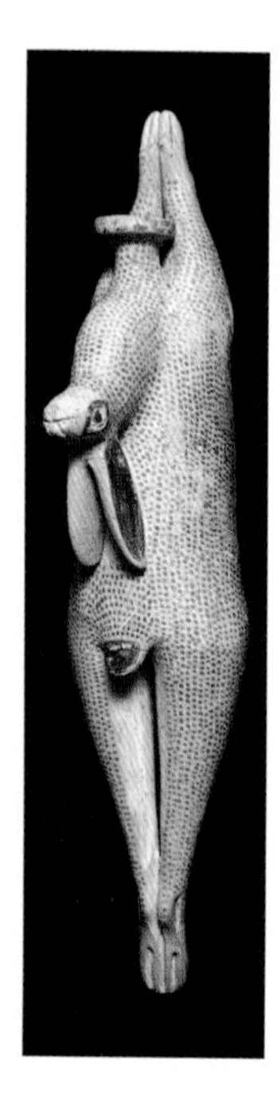

Zoomorphic Greek scent bottle, 6th century BC.

In India, in one of the Jataka stories reputed to have been told by the Buddha himself, Bodhisattva is born in one of his incarnations as a hare. In this form he preaches to several other animals the necessity of giving alms, and when they are visited by the god Sakka in the form of a hungry Brahmin, each of them offers food. But only the hare does so in an appropriate form, following the law that no life should be destroyed. He not only offers to sacrifice himself by leaping into a fire, but shakes his body three times to rid it of any creatures living in his fur. The offer is declined but, as a reward for his virtue, the incident is commemorated by the god by painting the hare's image on the moon. In another version the hare begins to carefully pick the insects from his fur in preparation for his death, and in a Sri Lankan version it is the Buddha himself who meets the self-sacrificing hare, rescues him from the fire and puts him on the moon. The connection between hares and fire is widespread, and has been explained by the fact that hares will stay in a burning field until the last moment (even, on occasion, catching fire), presumably due to their instinct, when confronted with danger, to use their speed as an ultimate rather than initial response. Layard says that we are dealing in this legend not with a real fire but with a version of that 'spiritual fire' which burns away all earthly dross.[15] What seems uppermost in the legend, though, is the hare's gentleness and its innocuousness as a prey species, a naturalistic basis for the purely Buddhist touch which has it avoiding the death even of its parasites before jumping into the fire. Though it should be added that, in another Jataka tale not mentioned by Layard, the timid hare plays a less admirable role, causing a panic in the animal kingdom by interpreting the thud made by a falling fruit as the beginning of the end of the world. The Buddha in the form of a lion averts disaster by halting the animals' stampede towards the sea.[16] A Tibetan folk-tale presents the hare in an even more unflattering light. For in it a hare blinds and kills a tiger, tells a man where he can find a tiger-skin, ravens where they can pick at the wounds on the man's now unattended horses, a shepherd where he can rob the raven's unattended nests, and a wolf where it can prey on the sheep left by the shepherd, before retiring to laugh so hard at the havoc caused that his lip was split.[17] Examples of such violent trickster-hares, with their

Rim of a Greek red-figured cup showing a live hare being given as a love-token, c. 490 BC.

'Trickster' hare and the King of the Elephants, illustration to a tale by Bidpai in Arabic translation, 1354.

usual reputation for gentleness or timidity reversed, can be found in African folklore and in tales of the Great Hare of the Algonquin Indians.

The moon-hare appears on early Buddhist family altars all over China. Chinese hare-moon symbolism is possibly derived from early Buddhist influence from India, though unique features are added there regarding the significance of coat colour, omens, 'political' significance and the (super)natural history of the creature. In a variation on the early naturalists' speculations on its peculiar reproductive system, and one which incorporates a version of immaculate conception, one authority says that the female becomes pregnant by gazing at the moon; another that it does so by licking the male's fur. In general the hare itself is said to derive its vital essence from the moon, and symbolically it is said to live there eternally compounding the elixir of life. Hence the many visual depictions of it on hind legs with pestle and mortar. In a Taoist fable it becomes the jade or gemmeous hare – a servitor of genii who employ it to compose the *elixir vitae*, and jade hare amulets are found in graves from the fourth century onwards.

As for colour symbolism, the white hare was given particular divine status. For Taoists it was thought to be the moon queen's servant, to live 1,000 years and to turn white after 500. Legends such as that of the 'golden age' of the Chou Dynasty, in which white hares were said to have played in the streets of the capital, can be seen to cut either way: as a religiously inflected interpretation of history, or as evidence pointing to an exploitation of popular belief by the Dynasts. The generally auspicious nature of the hare in China is further attested to by the fact that a red hare figures as a supernatural beast of auspicious omen, and a black one, as emissary of the moon goddess, was thought to be auspicious of a successful reign. A hare of unspecified colour was the second of the twelve emblems of the Emperor of China, and is said by one mythographer to be 'symbolic of the Yin force on the life of the monarch'.[18]

The taboo placed on eating hares by Judaism and early Christianity presents what the current *Catholic Encyclopedia* curtly terms 'a classical difficulty' without going into that difficulty, one which has been much discussed and interpreted. For how can a text purporting to be the direct word of God be wrong on a basic fact of natural history? The *Encyclopedia* sidesteps the difficulty by saying that hares *appear* to chew the cud, thus making them anomalous and 'unclean' amongst ungulates since they don't 'divide the hoof'.[19] Others have questioned whether *arnevet*, the original Hebrew, really refers to a hare, without convincingly bringing forward a more suitable referent, or argued that 'cheweth the cud' is really a reference to the fact that hares digest their food twice. Recent creationists, using this

Hare pounding mortar on Chinese bronze, AD 618–906.

interpretation, even go so far as to suggest that far from being wrong, Leviticus shows an understanding of the hare's digestive system which it took 'science' millennia to catch up with.[20] Such special pleading aside (and there is an entire book by a more credible Hebrew scholar: *The Camel, the Hare and the Hyrax*) it's not difficult to see how an animal observed eating excreted pellets might be deemed unclean, but it is intriguing to see questions of faith and of religious symbolism as well as dietary law issuing, as it were, from the digestive system of a hare.

Two of the so-called Fathers of the Church dissolved the difficulty by giving a symbolic interpretation to the passage, though in doing so they relied upon more outlandishly mistaken beliefs about hares. According to the *Epistle of Barnabas*, what the Bible is really saying when it says 'Thou shalt not eat the hare' is '"Thou shalt not be a corrupter of boys, nor like unto such". Because the hare multiplies, year by year, the places of its

A bird of prey pecking a hare, on a star-shaped ceramic tile from Kubad Abad Palace, Turkey, early 13th century.

Hares berthed in the Ark with a snake, from the 10th-century manuscript *Beatus in Apocalipsin* by Emeterio the Monk.

conception; for as many years as it lives so many it has.'[21] It is obscurely put, but seems to rely on the belief that each *annus* brought the hare a supernumerary orifice or *anus*, making it by a tortuous symbolic leap a symbol of homosexuality. On the same track but with reference to the more widespread belief that hares changed their sex, Novatian in 'On the Jewish Meats' asserts that when Leviticus forbids the hare it does so in order to 'rebuke men deformed into women'.[22] The general Christian symbolic association of the hare with lust is given a specific slant by a medieval image of a monk pursuing a naked boy with the appended text, 'I am a monk, I behave like a hare.' Novatian also gives a non-literal reading to dividing the hoof, for animals that do so walk 'with the firm step of innocency' and 'tread the ways of righteousness'. Thus in the animals of the Bible, and in the actual animals in all their variety, 'a certain mirror of human life is established'.[23]

Given their inauspicious appearances in the Judaeo-Christian mirror (unclean, emblems of 'unnatural' and sinful sex) hares make a surprising number and variety of appearances in Christian iconography and discourse, eventually acquiring positive symbolic or metaphoric associations with Easter (both the Crucifixion and Resurrection); the Virgin birth; the salvation of sinners in the Church; the working of divine Providence in the natural world; the Trinity; the Biblical Flood; the persecution of the faithful. In certain illustrated editions of the *Haggadah* (a Jewish religious text that sets out the order of the Passover Seder) there is even a tradition of emblematizing the persecution and deliverance of the Jews with images of hunted hares.

As late as the eighth century, however, the Church was issuing literal-minded prohibitions against eating hares, and against their use in divination. The Christian rehabilitation of the symbolic hare, so to speak, stems from a passage in the Psalms (104: 18): 'The high hills are a refuge for the hedgehogs; and the rocks for the hares'; and from another in Proverbs (30: 26): 'The hares are but feeble folk, yet they make their refuge in the rocks'. In his *Expositions on the Psalms*, St Augustine gives an interpretation which was to become typical and widespread. The hedgehog is a sinner covered with the 'prickles' of sin, and 'in his timidity he is a hare'. The rock is 'the Lord', and by extension the Church in which sinners find refuge and redemption.[24] Medieval bestiaries reinforced and elaborated the interpretation. The thirteenth-century so-called Bodleian Bestiary, for instance, has it that 'the rock is Christ. It is written of Moses that he, the hare of the Lord, shall stand in the cleft of the rock, because he hoped for salvation through the passion of our Redeemer.'[25] Others go further, by utilizing the fact that hares can run faster uphill than down: 'Seek you likewise the rock, when the evil cur, the demon pursues you . . . If he sees you running downhill with your heart set on the earthly things of this world, he comes in ready pursuit, aided by the confusion of your thoughts. But let him see that you run along with the will of God, seeking the rock of our Lord Jesus Christ, climbing to the summit of virtue, then the dog will turn back.'[26]

Such readings feed into Renaissance iconography. In the background of Benozzo Gozzoli's (*c.* 1421–1497) painting *Journey of the Magi*, a hunted hare can be seen hiding in the cleft of a rock. Though Gozzoli's hare may also encode a reference to the persecution of the Church, or even a prefigurement of the Crucifixion and Resurrection, hares hunted by dogs provided a ready metaphor for the persecution of early Christians. Tertullian, for instance, writes that 'We ourselves, having been appointed for pursuit, are like hares being hemmed in', while 'heretics go about according to their wont'.[27] Such similes hardly depended upon a consideration for actual hares as 'victims' of the hunt, though St Francis, St Neot and St Monacella all saved hares from hunters, while St Hellier is even said to have 'reasoned' with a hare not to endanger its life by eating a farmer's cabbages. The *Haggadah* illustrations of hare hunting include ones which show them driven towards nets by dogs and hunters on horseback, only for the nets to miraculously lift in a second, companion image, leaving the dogs ensnared, in remarkable allusion to the Passover.

At some point the association between the hare as victim of the hunt and the persecution of the Church widened to include its ultimate victim, most spectacularly in such images as Taddeo Crivelli's (fl. 1451) depiction of St Jerome kneeling before the cross, kissing the feet of the crucified Christ. Prominent in the lower margin of the inset image there is a greyhound in pursuit of a hare. The motif of hound and hare in symbolic association with Christ may have been reinforced by such texts as the one in which the Bishop of Ambrose maintained that the hare was an appropriate symbol of the Resurrection, because the hare

·S· HIERONYMVS

changes coat-colour in winter.[28] It's likely, too, that the motif was ambivalent, 'unofficial', and not readily understood even by learned viewers of such images.

The sexual behaviour and peculiarity of hares cuts both ways in Christian symbolism: lustfulness and 'unnatural' proclivity on the one hand; on the other mysterious and 'miraculous' superfecundity and the ability of the female hare to conceive without the male, making it an appropriate symbol of the miraculous virgin birth, usually, though not always, in the form of a white hare. Perceptions of the mysterious fertility of hares, combined with its association with the Resurrection, must have fed into the northern and central European tradition of giving Easter eggs. In a complex chain of associations, these eggs were deemed to have been symbolically 'laid' or delivered by a hare, a tradition which survives in modified form in the figure of the Easter 'bunny'. (Though in Germany, where the tradition probably originated, this leporine bunny is still a hare.) In addition there is the well-known derivation by Bede of the word 'Easter' itself from the Anglian goddess Eostre. It has been argued that 'Eostre' is linked to the Saxon goddess Ostara, and that both are from the same root as Aurora, Eos and Ushas, the Sanskrit for dawn. And that since the month of April was called Eostur-monath, or Dawn Month, the pre-Christian festival of Easter must have included rites symbolic of death and resurrection. As Jacob Grimm was to write, on Ostara: 'she is the divinity of the radiant dawn, of upspringing light, a spectacle that brings joy and blessing, and whose meaning could easily be adapted to the resurrection of the Christian God'.[29]

Clinching the connection between Eostre and Easter in northern Europe, it is also frequently asserted that the goddess's favourite animal and attendant spirit was the hare. Layard concludes that the Easter hare and its eggs are a survival of what at

Taddeo Crivelli, *St Jerome in the Desert*, with hound and hare motif prominent, *c.* 1469. Tempera colours, gold paint, gold leaf and ink on parchment.

one time must have been an organized ritual in honour of 'the hare-goddess'. Convincing as all this seems, though, the only evidence even for the existence of the goddess Eostre is Bede's, who has nothing to say about her attributes or totem animal. Eostre's connection with the hare might even be a piece of twentieth-century folklore designed to invest the Christian festival with colourfully pagan roots. Be that as it may, the connection between hares and Easter eggs is firmly established, and has been recorded in Austria, Czechoslovakia, Hungary and neighbouring lands. Sometimes the painted hollow eggs have windows through which can be seen, inside the egg, a picture of Christ rising from the tomb, or of some other related religious subject.

Other Christian uses of the hare include its prominence in certain Creation scenes in illuminated texts, such as the one in which it appears second in line only to the elephant. Its presence in depictions of the biblical Flood is possibly derived from the legend that the hare used its foot in order to plug a hole in the ark, thus saving its human and other creaturely cargo. In a variation on the theme it uses its tail, which is cut off, thus accounting for the fact that hares do not have 'proper' tails. Numerous appearances of hares feeding on grapes or foliage in ornamental details in churches have been interpreted as representing souls in heaven. Sometimes the foliage is trifoliate, as in Cashel Cathedral, with an obvious allusion to the Trinity. Occasionally the motif also incorporates an eagle, as in a particularly elaborate Italian example that has been interpreted in the following way: 'The two hares (that often have a negative meaning) in this case represent the sinners who find their shelter and redemption in Christ. The eagle holding the Eucharist grapes is clearly a reference to the resurrected and victorious Christ 'who opened the arms like wings on the Cross, who brought salvation thanks to his sacrifice'.[30]

In many bosses on the ceilings of parish churches in Devon and Cornwall, as well as in a stained glass window in Paderborn Cathedral in Germany, there is a motif of three hares running in a ring, linked by their ears, and this has also been interpreted as an allusion to the indissoluble unity of Father, Son and Holy Ghost. Though as recent researchers have discovered, it's an ancient motif which also occurs in Buddhist China and in Iran.[31] In contexts, that is, separated by thousands of miles and 500 years. In other English churches figurative representations can be found not only of hares in association with the Virgin Mary and with sinners seeking refuge in the 'rock' of Christ, but attendant upon a depiction of David slaying Goliath. The latter has been interpreted with reference to the fact that David is an Old Testament 'type' of Christ, slaying Goliath or Satan in order to deliver the watching army of Israelites (the hares).[32] Less eccentrically, there are also instances of eagles killing hares in carved stone and wooden details in such churches, in reference to 'the defeat of lust, the Hare, by Christ the Eagle', as one recent writer on church carvings has it.[33] This negative association between hares and lustfulness is particularly prevalent in medieval texts and images, surviving into the Renaissance in variously altered and elaborated forms.

Other positive appearances of hares in Christian texts include their role as exempla of divine providence manifesting itself in every detail of the Creation. St Basil, in a passage demonstrating that 'beasts bear witness to the faith' reflects upon the fact that 'the easiest animals to catch are the most productive', and explains that 'it is on account of this that hares and goats produce many little ones, for fear these species should disappear . . . Thus in nature all has been foreseen, all is the object of continual care.'[34] In homiletic literature another naturalistic observation of the hare – namely its exceptional speed – provides an exemplum

against the sin of pride. Are you proud of 'the swiftness of thy feet?' asks St John Chrysostom: 'Again the first prize is with unreasoning animals, the hare, and the gazelle . . .'.[35] Conversely, when seeking to demonstrate 'that the Demons are not better than Men because of their aerial bodies' in *The City of God*, St Augustine has occasion to ask rhetorically 'Who can equal the hare, the stag, and all the birds in their swiftness?'[36] Compared to the hare and other species of God's creation, the 'Demons' have inferior powers even of locomotion.

The hare second in order to the elephant, in a scene depicting the creation of the animals on earth, from a 13th-century bestiary.

Some of the marginal images of hares that appear in Christian contexts (on the borders of illuminated texts, in carvings within and on the outside of churches and cathedrals, on vestments and other objects) can be explained with reference to 'official sources'. But they also partake of that swarming, riddling, open-ended and 'unofficial' visual activity that occurs in the borders of medieval and Gothic art. In the Bury Bible, for instance, painted for the monks of Bury St Edmunds around 1130, the very first letter of the book contains a riot of figures including a

Four hares with linked ears, an illustration from a 13th-century bestiary.

centaur, a fish-tailed siren and a man with a wooden leg attempting to shave a hare with scissors. A recent historian and theorist of such marginal figures has explained this latter image as deriving from a popular riddle concerning impossibility (the unlikelihood of a man with a wooden leg being able to catch a hare, let alone shave it with scissors) and categorized it as an *adynaton* – a representation of an impossible task.[37] Given its prominence on the first page of the text, he goes on to ask: 'Is this a pictorial gloss on the difficulty of reading itself, of pinning down the meaning of the biblical text itself?' This is ingeniously put, and whatever our response to the question, the process of arriving at it mirrors the nature of the problems that were playfully set for their readers by the creators of such images. Problems which did not always have such coherent solutions, and which were not always appreciated or understood even by those for whom they were explicitly intended. There are several instances of early complaints about the irruption of animal imagery into sacred contexts and spaces. The Cistercian Aelred of Rievaulx, for instance, writes of how 'in the monastic cloister we see cranes and hares, deeres, stags, magpies and crows'. According to Aelred, these do not accord with monastic spirituality. They are, rather, 'more like the amusements of women'.[38]

The Christian association of the hare with lustfulness was as nothing to the role the creature was to play in the persecution of witchcraft in England in the sixteenth and seventeenth centuries. The grounds for the witch-craze were prepared by a general Protestant turn against survivals of paganism and superstition. As early as the twelfth century the belief is recorded, by Giraldus Cambrensis, that 'certain hags in Wales as well as Scotland changed into hares to suck the teats of neighbours' cattle'.[39] Sir Walter Scott, among others, attests to the survival of belief in the witch-hare into the nineteenth century; Evans and

Thomson cite oral accounts showing its survival even into the 1970s. A document relating to the trial of one of the chief Lancashire witches of 1613 provides an instance of the collision between Church, superstition and law, centred upon a supernatural hare. In it James Device confessed:

> that upon Shrove Tuesday was two years, his Grand-Mother Elizabeth Sotherness, alias Devilsdike, did bid him this Examinate goe to the Church to receive the Communion (the next day after being Good Friday) and then not to eate the Bread the Minister gave him, but to bring it and deliver it to such a thing as should meet him in his way homewards. Notwithstanding her persuasions, the Examinate did eate the Bread; and so in his comming homeward some fortie roods of the saide Church, there met him a thing in the shape of a Hare, who spoke unto this Examinate, and asked him whether hee had brought the Bread.[40]

It is a remarkable passage, in which the kind of precision appropriate to a courtroom ('some fortie roods') is combined with absurd credulity (the talking, uncanny hare), an admission of culpability with an actual shifting of guilt onto the old woman, and above all for the way in which it seems explicitly constructed to confirm the worst suspicions of the examiners: by confirming a plot to misappropriate the power of the Church by literally stealing the bread of Communion. It is a confession not of paganism but of inverted belief in the power of the sacrament, the actual bread that can become the body of Christ.

It is not clear whether the hare or 'thing in the shape of a hare' in this case is meant to be the unfortunate grandmother or the devil himself. In another part of his confession, Device testifies to having seen a hare 'spitting fire', and there is at least one period visual depiction of 'Beelzebub' with head of a tiger and ears of hare. Usually, though, it was the witch herself that 'went into' a hare. A variation on the theme sees her hunted by hounds while transformed, only to turn back into a woman as she is caught. Bite marks are left on her now human body, however, rather than being erased during its resumption. Yeats gives a version of this scenario in the form of a folk-tale.[41] But in the world of the witch-trials such marks could be pointed to as damningly conclusive (like the presence on the body of a supernumerary nipple), in a grim travesty of 'forensic' evidence. In a notorious Scottish trial Isobel Gowdie confessed to having regularly assumed the form of a hare, even providing examples of spells to be uttered to 'go into' one, and to resume human shape, before concluding with a confirmation of the witch-finders' pseudo-forensic assumptions: 'the dogs will sometimes get bits of us, but will not get us killed. And when we turn to our own shape, we will have bits, and rives, and scarts in our bodies.'[42] Not that even this much 'evidence', probably extracted under torture, was required. Julian Coxe was convicted because she was seen out of breath behind a hedge through which a hunted hare had vanished. Her breathlessness was taken as fatal evidence of her transformation into the form of a hare.[43]

Why the hare, in this context? Naturalistic explanations include the fact that it is nocturnal, solitary, somewhat mysterious, popularly (and learnedly) believed to be lascivious; sometimes seen in 'parliaments' or sitting in coven-like circles with other hares. It has also been suggested that, like the cat, the hare is singled out as a 'human-in-disguise' because it 'usurps the right to stare'.[44] By assuming its form, witches were probably also thought to be usurping some of the positive associations the animal had acquired as a symbol in Christianity, stolen away and inverted like the host in the testimony by James Device. Or rather, stolen back, since in northern Europe, at any rate, Christianity tapped into the power the hare derived from Celtic and British paganism. According to Dio the ancient Britons not only tabooed hare flesh (a sure sign of a sacred function) but used hares for the purpose of divination. Boudicca is said by him to have released a live hare on the field of battle for some such purpose.

The presence of hares in sacred and mythological contexts in Latin America is somewhat confusing and confused. One of the earliest interpreters of Mesoamerican culture, Bernardino de Sahagún, thought that the Mexica derived their very name from the god Mexitli or Mecitli, and that Mecitli means 'hare (*citli*) of the agave (*metl*)'.[45] Sahagún, a Franciscan missionary, arrived in Mexico less than a decade after the conquest of 1521, and it's possible that his interpretation was influenced by Christian animal symbolism. Modern scholars, at any rate, suggest as translations for Mexico 'Place of the Navel of the Moon' or 'Place of the Navel of the Agave'. Both hares and rabbits are associated with the moon in Mayan and Aztec iconography – no doubt because of the resemblance of the dark patches or *maria* of the moon to a lagomorph – but little clear distinction seems to have been made between the symbolic valences of the two creatures. Modern interpretation has not been helped by the fact that those doing the interpreting tend to work with scant sense of the basic actual differences between the two animals. A passage from Michael Graulich's *Myths of Ancient Mexico* is unusual inasmuch as it even acknowledges the problem, but typical inasmuch as it rapidly reveals a confused sense of the natural history of hares:

> Moon and Venus seem to have been confused. Citli, 'hare' or 'grandmother', as Venus is called in Mendieta, is a

Pre-Columbian effigy vessel, Mexico.

> name that seems more suited to the moon. For Mexicans, a hare and a rabbit, the animal in the moon, were the same, even if they are really different animals. A hare is as swift as Ehecatl, another name for Venus. It lives in a burrow [*sic*], which is a cave in the earth, and its excrement resembles maize kernels. The hare resembles the moon, who entered a cave, and also Cinteotl-Venus, who buried himself and was changed into maize.[46]

Hares, of course, do not live in burrows, though it's possible that ancient Mesoamericans may have observed the not unusual phenomenon of jackrabbits sheltering from the sun in burrows made by other animals. (*Burrowing* is crucial in this context, because it gives the animal connection to the underworld.) If there is really no distinction to be made in Mesoamerican symbolization and myth between the hare and the rabbit (even though a linguistic distinction was made, as recorded in Sahagún's Nahuatl dictionary, the earliest of its kind) then it gives licence to interpret the presence of the hare in such contexts as the eighth of the twenty day-symbols in the Aztec calendar; in the Huastec Maya myth in which a rabbit warned people of the coming of a great flood that would destroy the world (when the deluge came, the rabbit-hare boarded a boat and disembarked on the moon); in the nomenclature of the Aztec pantheon of deities ('400 rabbits'); and in the Mayan texts and images which associate a lagomorph with the idea of writing.[47] Both rabbits and hares were hunted by Mesoamericans for their flesh and fur, with skins used also as a kind of 'tribute' currency. In Aztec medicine, also, according to one recent authority, they were frequently used and interchangeable in remedies related to their 'speed and agility'.[48]

The most direct and developed sacred use of a hare figure occurred north of the border between modern Mexico and the United States, though since native American religion and myth was orally transmitted as well as fluid and subject to tribal variations, our scant knowledge of its earliest forms is significantly dependent upon the reports of missionaries and colonists. In 1610 an official of the colony of Virginia questioned several Indians about their religion.

> We have 5 godes in all, our chief god appears often unto us in the likewise of a mightie great Hare . . . our God who takes upon this shape of a Hare conceaved with himself how to people this great world, and with what kind of

> Creatures, and yt is true (said he) that at length he divised and made divers men and women and made provision for them to be kept up yet for a whyle in a great bag . . .[49]

This 'Great Hare' or 'chimerical beast' as one of the missionaries called it, figured centrally in the religion of the geographically widespread Algonquin tribes, including the Powhatans of Virginia, the Lenni Lenape of the Delaware, various tribes of New England, as well as western tribes and the Ottawa of the far north. In another early recorded testimony, as reported by one of the first French missionaries to arrive, the Ottawa were said to have been formed by three families, the first that of the Great Hare who, after forming the earth was inspired by a spider to invent fishing nets, and who set forth burial rights for his descendants. Other early and subsequent accounts expanded upon the Great Hare's role as both principal deity and culture hero, crediting him with the creation of habitable land from a grain of sand taken from the bottom of the ocean; the invention of picture-writing and of many charms and signs used in the hunt (and even of originally sorting game from non-game species) as well as founding the culturally important 'medicine society' or Meda.

By the time anthropologists such as Paul Radin (1883–1959) began to more systematically collect oral and other evidence of native American religion, it was clear that the Algonquian hare deity had metamorphosed over time, and that missionaries had done more than simply record its existence. They had in fact eventually contributed to a kind of syncretism or Christianizing of the hare. In his book *The Winnebago Tribe* Radin reveals how members of the Winnebago Peyote Cult came to identify the Great Hare with Christ. And how emphasis was given, in the absence of written sacred texts, to oral transmission. This is how one of the Winnebago conveys his understanding of the

Aztec vessel in the form of a hare, probably used to contain chocolate.

Great Hare in general, and the medicine dance in particular, in the early 1920s: 'A grandmother of mine was the cause of it. She said that the Creator's son was called the Hare; that he came on earth and brought life, she said. She said that whoever did this (medicine dance) would live well, that their souls would always return to the place where the Creator sits . . . They, the medicine men, were repeating what the Hare had done.'[50] A more general and systematic account of the Winnebago in Ruth M. Underhill's *Red Man's Religion* suggests that they bisected the older deity under the influence of Christianity, with the Creator responding to man's unhappiness by sending down Hare in human form as a saviour.[51] Combining the ideas of immaculate conception and the necessity of actual kinship with human beings, Hare enters the womb of a virgin. With Christlike, supernatural compassion he hears when still in the womb the weeping and shrieking of people beset by 'the evil ones', but with native vigour bursts out of her body prematurely, thus killing his mother. Having destroyed the evil ones and thrust them down under the earth, his grandmother (earth or fertility) produced corn and tobacco from her body. Then he bestowed the final gift put in his power by the Creator, the power over life and death, which he enabled them to achieve by establishing the medicine lodge.

The Winnebago, together with the other Algonquin tribes, also figured the hare as a kind of trickster, about whose exploits many tales were told. One recent authority convincingly summarizes his exploits as having to do with fighting 'what may be called arrogation', as when Grasshopper arrogates to himself tobacco, or when a single bad spirit arrogated to himself all the possessions of mankind.[52] It also takes no leap of the historical imagination to see such fables as coded echoes or offshoots of

Mimbres ceramic bowl depicting black-tailed jackrabbit above the crescent moon, AD 1000–1150.

the seminal 'arrogation' in native American history: the appropriation of tribal territories. Or to see that history echoed in more pessimistic legends than the one in which the Hare secures the lasting happiness of mankind, or rescues women from the Spirit of Gambling which held them captive, or kills a man-eating monster by having himself swallowed by it before cutting himself out of its belly with a sharpened flint. In one such tale Hare has the opportunity to ward off death from human beings altogether – if he could only walk a perfect circle around the world without looking back at his grandmother. But he was unable to resist the backward look.

Folk tales involving the hare as a kind of trickster-hero also abound in Africa. Historians of African literature have described the range of his appearances as even more 'continental' than that of Ananse, probably the best-known of the African tricksters. Though not part of religious discourse narrowly defined, one such southern African tale (recorded in several variants) deals with nothing less than the origins of human mortality, or failure to possess immortality, and plays a variation upon the widespread sacred and lunar associations of the animal. The ant is sent by the moon to give to mankind the message 'as I die and then rise again, so shall you'. But the ant is met by a hare who rebukes him for carrying his message so slowly, before taking over the role of messenger himself, only to deliver it in a form with a meaning opposite to that intended: 'as I die and do not rise again, so shall you'. The moon strikes the hare, splitting its lip. In many of the tales the hare exhibits a cunning and intelligence which allows him to outwit more powerful opponents, but there are a significant number in which the animal also exhibits anarchic unreliability and even a capacity for extreme violence, albeit violence answering that offered to it, tendencies which give him a family resemblance to the North American trickster hare. In one of these a man coerces the hare into making a pact to kill their mothers, but the hare hides his mother and siblings in the sky. When the man, having already committed matricide, discovers this, he finds and kills them in their hiding place. In revenge the hare persuades him to lie down to receive a present of cooked meat, only to place in his mouth instead a red-hot stone, thus killing him. [53]

The symbolic richness of this tale defies interpretation, or at any rate the kind of culturally non-specific interpretation which seeks in myth and folklore 'universal' truths. Animal fables transmitted orally from the time of Aesop were later tagged with *epimythia* or concluding 'morals' for universal application, in a process which can serve here to illustrate the taming of the tale itself, and the ways in which such *epimythia* were determined by the concerns of those constructing them. The hare appears in many fables of Greek and Roman origin, including in its race with the tortoise, probably the most well known of all beast fables. 'The Hare and the Tortoise' has had an intriguing afterlife, from schoolbook illustration of the Protestant work ethic ('slow and sure wins the race') to Ambrose Bierce's dissenting definition of 'perseverance' as 'a lowly virtue whereby mediocrity achieves an inglorious success', a definition which he illustrates with verses describing the losing lepus: 'Where is the hare . . . / He sleeps, like a saint in a holy place,/ A winner of all that is good in a race.'[54] And from Malthus's use of it to argue how population increase must be arrested or 'put to sleep' (like the hare), in order to allow limited food resources (the tortoise) to catch up with it,[55] to a recent work of pop psychology, *Hare Brain, Tortoise Mind,* with the attractive sub-title *How Intelligence Increases When You Think Less.*[56] In the context of its original Greek telling it would probably have mattered that it was a tale of an underdog (universally preyed upon

Dogon ceremonial, *Hare/Antelope* mask, West Mali, 1940s.

creature) outdone by a greater underdog and that the victory achieved over the hare was by way of circumventing its greatest power, its speed. Add to the mix the fact that Aesop was a freed slave, and that the hare was associated with 'aristocratic' hunting, and a political subtext can be glimpsed. Different *epimythia* given to the same fable, at any rate, directly reflect the historical concerns of those devising them in a way that complicates their claims to 'universality'. In 'The Hare and the Frogs', hares about to commit suicide by jumping into a pond (because they can no longer bear their fearful existence) change their minds on seeing startled frogs jump in ahead of them. They are not the

Gustave Doré's illustration to La Fontaine's version of *The Hares and the Frogs*.

most 'timorous' after all. In the first English printing of Aesop in 1484 the reader is directed to conclude that 'therefore in the unhappy and Infortunat tyme men ought not to be despaired but ought ever to be in good hope to have one better in tyme of prosperyte. For after grete were cometh good Pees. And after the raine coemeth the fair weder.'[57] It is a conclusion imbued with Christian sentiment and a medieval feeling for the metaphorical and actual power of seasonal change, of 'due season' as well as one which links personal with national 'travail'. By the time of Roger L'Estrange's equally influential Aesop edition of 1692, the moral had morphed to show that 'there's no contending with the Orders and Decrees of Providence. He that made us knows what's fittest for us; and every Man's own Lot (well understood and managed) is undoubtedly the best.'[58] This Christian exhortation to the reader to *know your place* barely masks a politically conservative message devised for readers for whom the Civil War was not a remote memory. Sticking rather more closely to the action of the fable itself, a recent translation appends a moral imbued with a distinctly modern and psychologizing sense of *Schadenfreude*: 'Unhappy people are comforted by the sight of someone who is worse off than they are'.[59] As in fables, so in myth. John Layard, in his influential essay on 'The Mythology of the Hare', saw the hare running all roads to and from the Collective Unconscious, where Jung had placed it as an archetype.[60] It seems more likely that it was arising, then morphing, in response to particular cultural and historical concerns and situations.

3 Hunted Hare

When in 2004 the British parliament banned the hunting of hares with dogs (thus bringing English and Welsh law in line with earlier bans instituted in Scotland and Northern Ireland, as well as in most other European countries),[1] it must have seemed to many like a quaint footnote or side-issue to the banning of the more vexed, central and 'traditional' sport of fox-hunting, though not to those supporters of the Waterloo Cup, a three-day coursing event which originated in 1836 and which regularly drew up to 10,000 spectators to watch and bet on pairs of greyhounds competing against each other in pursuit of hares, with a complex set of rules substantially based on those established during the reign of Elizabeth I. The rules awarded points for such manoeuvres by the dogs as 'The Wrench', 'The Turn' and 'The Go-Bye' as well as for the self-explanatory 'Trip' and 'Kill'. Or to the members of that residual number of hunts which pursued hares on horseback with harriers or beagles, or on foot behind bassets. Hunting hares with harriers has been described as 'fox-hunting in miniature', but it's a phrase that occludes the historical precedence of hare-hunting. It was not until the mid-nineteenth century that the number of packs of foxhounds in England exceeded that of harriers. Considered in a wider and longer perspective, the formalized chasing of hares for sport is much older and has been accorded more central importance in the literature of hunting, and in anti-hunting discourses. And since the hare was classified early in law as one of the principal 'game' species (rather than, like the fox, as 'vermin'), it has figured prominently in that series of punitive legislations regarding 'qualification' to take it – a royal prerogative extended to the aristocracy and then to the land-owning classes – which have significantly shaped the social histories of some of the major European nations.

The earliest extant hunting treatise is composed as if almost everything that can be said about the art can be done so by considering the pursuit of hares with hounds. For Xenophon, roughly 70 per cent of whose *Cynegeticus* or 'Hunting with Hounds' is about hare hunting, the hare is the quintessential quarry, virtually synonymous with the pleasures of the chase – 'so pleasing, that whoever sees it trailed, or found, or pursued, or taken, forgets everything he is most attached to.'[2] For this retired Greek general writing in the fourth century BC, as for later theorists of the hunt, it is the hare's combination of speed, endurance and 'artfulness' that makes it so suitable for sport. A sport which consisted of following on foot what must have been relatively slow-moving scent-hounds, for he writes that 'she is not overtaken by the dogs by speed alone, she is so fast; if they are caught, it is in spite of their natural physique, by accident.'[3] Xenophon's text is remarkable for the way in which it represents hunting as an education in myth (beginning with a discourse on the origins of hunting with the gods, and its beneficial effects on certain heroes) and an inculcator of martial and *polis* or citizenship values (framed in an argument against the sophists, a school of philosophers he accuses of self-interest), but it is also a foundational text for the priority which it gives to hunting as pleasure and as sport rather than as a means of securing food. Hunting, even or especially the hunting of hares, 'promotes good physical health, improves sight and hearing, delays old age, and especially trains men for war'.[4] But nowhere is the alimentary value or utility of the animals hunted even so much as mentioned, despite the fact that there are no fewer than seventeen recipes for hare flesh recorded by Apicius.

Hares were released on islands throughout the Aegean for the purpose of hunting, and large enclosures were also developed to protect them from predators. The Egyptians and Romans also utilized such enclosures, and the Roman writer Varro writes of how the 'leporaria' or game reserves on country estates of late Republican times were so called because 'our remote ancestors' kept only hares in them.[5] Xenophon's text exemplifies the conversion of hunting for food into a sporting, symbolic and warlike activity, with the hare particularly valued for its ability to 'work' a pack of hounds to the maximum degree. In another of the most important hunting treatises to survive from classical times, Arrian's *Cynegeticus*, hare-hunting is also given central importance. Arrian reprises many of Xenophon's themes and hunting methods, with addition of the consideration of the use of faster dogs. He also introduces a note that further removes the hare from any utilitarian function, by putting into question the very idea that the object of the hunt should be to actually catch and kill it. While agreeing with Xenophon that 'the sight of the creature being found, pursued and hunted would drive thoughts of love from the mind of a lover', Arrian is of the opinion that 'to see her caught is neither a pleasant sight nor exciting, but upsetting rather'.[6] Though on the face of it a curiously self-contradictory sentiment, it was one that was to be echoed in various forms in later writing on venery with regard to the hare: from the would-be chivalric notion that the animal should not be 'overmatched' by its pursuers, to claims regarding both hunting with harriers and coursing with greyhounds that hares

Roman mosaic depicting a hare taken by a hunter on foot with a spear, Piazza Armerina, Sicily, early 4th century.

are rarely if ever actually killed by either 'sport'. One twentieth-century writer on hare hunting even claims, most implausibly, to have followed the hounds for twenty years without having seen a hare killed.[7]

Roman fondness for hare hunting is testified to by the fact that, wherever possible, they introduced populations of wild hares into conquered territories. In addition to their role in the formalized, sportive and aristocratic kind of hunting described by Arrian, they were hunted or more straightforwardly taken for food. Virgil, in his *Georgics*, advises farmers in winter to chase 'long-eared hares'.[8] In addition to the use of dogs in *par*

Lombard pattern-book illustration of a hound coursing a hare, *c.* 1400, pen and ink and water-colour with white heightening on parchment.

force hunting, there is visual evidence showing that they hunted hares with spears and other weapons, just as the Greeks apparently employed a throwing-stick called a *lagobolon*. In the mosaics in the Roman villa at Piazza Armerina in Sicily there is a depiction of a spear-carrying hunter on foot holding a dead hare, and another of a child running a spear through the chest of a curiously outsized hare, suggesting that this particular quarry, when enclosed, could have served by way of apprenticeship to bloodier and more 'dangerous' pursuits. It is an image at some remove from the delicate scruples of Arrian, or from Martial's favourite 'turn' at the circus: lions trained to 'play' with hares without harming them. Concerning the sport's aristocratic standing when undertaken with hounds, however, and its arduousness (one of the factors making it 'good training for war'), Horace advises a friend to join a wealthy patron when hunting for either boar or hares, for the sport 'will help your reputation, your health, your muscles and your circulation'.[9] In a version of the 'divertingness' of hare hunting differently inflected from that of Xenophon's, Ovid even suggests it as a palliative for a jilted lover. For at night, after a day spent pursuing

Child spearing a hare in the *Little Hunt* mosaic, Piazza Armerina, Sicily, early 4th century.

'with a clever hound the cowering hare', 'sleep, not longing for your girl, will overcome you'.[10]

The high standing accorded to hare hunting in the classical world was echoed in medieval and Renaissance Europe. Gaston Phebus writes of the hare that hunting it is more pleasurable than hunting any other animal in the world,[11] and gives five reasons why this is so, including the fact that a hunted hare will proceed 'so subtly and maliciously', running fast and with stamina but also employing various ingenious ruses to confuse its scent trail and the pursuing hounds. In seven separate illustrations to his *Livre de Chasse* hares are depicted in fully fledged hunting for sport: in one being pursued by a mixture of mounted hunters and others on foot, with a combination of scent-hounds and sight-hounds, in another being coursed with fine greyhounds. A third is notable for what it reveals of the parallel history or underside of aristocratic hunting, for it shows two illegal hunters transgressing one of the rules of chivalric hunting by using nets to catch hares on uncultivated ground. And should there be any doubt as to the nature of their criminality, the illustrator has given the poachers faces contorted with 'villainy'.[12]

In England, where the hare's standing seems if anything to have been even higher, the hare is described in *The Master of Game* (a work adapted from Phebus which alters the chapter-order to put hare-hunting first) as 'king of all venery',[13] and in the *Boke of St Albans* as 'the marvellest beest that is in any londe'.[14] For the author of *The Master of Game* the hare is not only transformed from lowly prey to 'king', but the hunting of it is seen as at the origins of all sophisticated *par force* hunting, 'for blowing and the fair terms of hunting cometh of the seeking and finding of the hare'. These fifteenth-century texts were central to the theory and practice of aristocratic and chivalric hunting, with

'Unsporting' poaching of hares, from the *Livre de Chasse* by Gaston Phebus.

its elaborate procedures, preparation and specialized vocabulary, and hare hunting *par force* (without weapons) provided a microcosm of the most complex aspects of the medieval chase. A hundred years later, in George Gascoigne's *The Noble Art of Venerie or Hunting*, the hare was still being written about in superlative terms as the most elusive and cunning of opponents, even when found and nearly matched for speed by the greyhound rather than the harrier or a similar scent-hound. For Gascoigne the hare 'maketh greatest pastime and pleasure, and sheweth most cunning in hunting, and is meetest for gentlemen of all other huntings'.[15] Even Peter Beckford's late eighteenth-century *Thoughts On Hunting*, a work which enshrined in print the newly widespread English sport of fox-hunting, has occasion to remark on how, 'as far as her own safety is concerned', the hare 'has more cunning than the fox, and makes many shifts to save her life far beyond all his artifice'. Beckford describes one such 'shift' – the sideways spring which the brown hare will make to break its scent trail – as 'hardly to be credited, any more than her ingenuity in making it: both are wonderful'. Like Xenophon, Arrian and Phebus before him, Beckford is also

Hare hunting on foot and on horseback, with sight- and scent-hounds, from the late 15th-century *Livre de Chasse* by Gaston Phebus.

A hare as big as a hound, in a mixed hunting scene painted on a late sixteenth-century Bohemian glass drinking vessel.

moved to concede the hare's greater suitability in 'working' to the maximum a pack of hounds, for 'if you really love to see your hounds hunt, the hare, when properly hunted, will show more of it than any other animal'.[16]

Gascoigne also praises hare hunting for its capacity to 'represent' other activities, noting that the 'nimble Hare, by turning in hir course,/Doth plainly prove that Pollicie, sometime surpasseth force'.[17] For him as for the other medieval and Renaissance theorists of venery and their classical precursors, however, it was valued for its promotion of 'manly', including martial, virtues – a notion echoed as late as Beckford, who writes of the hunting of hares as 'a manly and a wholesome exercise' which 'seems by Nature designed to be the amusement of a Briton'. It should be noted, however, that there was also a tendency, originating in the late sixteenth century and embodied in particularly virulent form in the person of James I of England, of belittling hare coursing in particular for being less 'manly' and martial than the *par force* pursuit of more dangerous quarry such as the stag or boar. In *The Booke Named the Governour*, Thomas Elyot writes in macho-aristocratic style that 'Hunting of the hare with greyhounds is right good solace for men that be studious, of them to whom nature hath not given personage or courage for the wars. And also for gentlewomen which fear neither sun nor wind for impairing their beauty. And peradventure they shall be thereat less idle than they should be at home in their chambers.'[18]

In one respect, though, the theorists of hunting as a ritualized aristocratic privilege were in agreement. For what conceptually distinguished gentlemanly, chivalric and 'legitimate' hunting from 'hunting for the pot' lies precisely in its construction as pure pleasure, an activity with any kind of associated benefit as long as it is not merely utilitarian. Addressing a patron, and echoing Horace, in his poem 'To Sir Robert Wroth', Ben Jonson depicts him typically hunting 'the flying hare,/ More for thy exercise than fare.'[19] This emphasis on the non-utilitarian essence of hunting seems designed to exclude at a theoretical level, and to justify, the exclusion of the masses from hunting that was enshrined in law. What can't be over-emphasized is how the kinds of hunting celebrated in medieval and Renaissance treatises were the exclusive privileges of a particular class, as much so with regard to hares as to deer. For as James I succinctly put it, 'it is not fit that clowns should have such sports'.[20]

In England 'clowns' or peasants were excluded from taking hares from the time of the Norman Forest Laws. And not just peasants, for game was the exclusive privilege of the king before it was granted to the aristocratic and land-owning classes. According to the *Anglo-Saxon Chronicle*, William the Conqueror not only forbade the killing of deer and wild boar, but 'likewise . . . decreed by the hares, that they should go free. His rich men bemoaned it, and the poor men shuddered at it.'[21] A statute issued under the reign of Richard II prohibited 'laymen' from even *keeping* greyhounds, and from catching hares in nets or snares unless possessed of lands or tenements with a specific high annual income, under pain of a year's imprisonment. One of Wat Tyler's revolutionary demands during the Great Revolt of 1381 was that all warrens, parks and chases should be free, 'so that throughout the realm, in . . . the woods and forests, poor as well as rich might take wild beasts and hunt the hare in the field'.[22] Clearly what was at stake here, and remained so for centuries to come, was rather more than the exquisite pleasure of venery. Richard II's game statute was produced in direct response to the Revolt, and couched in terms which made an explicit link between sedition and the demands of servants and labourers to hunt. For 'sometimes under such colour' (that is, while out hunting) such servants and labourers 'make their assemblies, conferences and conspiracies for to rise and disobey their allegiance'.[23]

So the killing of a hare by an 'unqualified' person became not only an illegal act punishable under the law, but one which was tantamount to sedition. It was an equation which was to be echoed down the centuries, and especially in the eighteenth and nineteenth centuries, not least by Thomas Carlyle, who maintained that the *French Revolution itself* was 'made by the poachers of France'.[24] Game privilege was indeed one of the first laws swept away in France, and the increasingly punitive game laws devised in England in the eighteenth and nineteenth centuries were no doubt partly motivated by the notion that their relaxation would be the first step on the road to revolution. Though it looks eccentric at first sight, Carlyle's assertion was actually in the mainstream of a certain strain of conservative thinking about the link between game privilege and the preservation of the *anciens régimes*; between its reform and the unravelling of the social order. And it was not just Carlyle who felt the social and political importance of game law elsewhere in Europe. For according to the editors of the *Collected Works* of Karl Marx, his first explicitly political rather than philosophical essay was written directly after reporting as a journalist on the proceedings of the Rhine Province Assembly, including on one session in which a law was passed 'depriving the peasantry of even the right to hunt hares'.

In England the deprivation of that right can be traced in some detail through its game laws.[25] Though such laws covered a number of animals, including the precious deer, the hare was one of the commonest 'poached' – a ready meal relatively easy to take at night with snare and long-dog – and therefore one leading to the greatest number of prosecutions. Under Richard II an income from lands worth an annual 40 shillings was required to hunt a hare. By 1604 no one with less than ten pounds annually – or 'of good family' – was legally entitled to own a greyhound. In a proclamation made towards the end of her reign, Elizabeth I declared that all game 'belongeth to the men of the best sort and condition'. James I and his successors referred to hares, partridges and pheasants as 'the King's game', and appointed royal gamekeepers for entire counties. The attempt by Charles I to revive the forest laws in the 1630s was reversed by the Long Parliament and the outbreak of civil war. The restoration of the forest laws in 1660 as a source of crown patronage and symbol of the power of the monarchy was reinforced in 1671 by the Game Act. This forbade all persons to hunt game unless they had freeholds worth £100 a year, or leaseholds worth £150 a year. To put this in context, it meant that you required to hunt a hare an income 50 times that of the electoral franchise. The Act, which remained in force for the next 160 years (with changes only to punishments meted out) effectively excluded those with non-landed wealth from the ranks of qualified sportsmen, as much as those with no wealth, and transferred the game prerogative from the king to the landed gentry.

Historians are divided as to how rigorously game laws were prosecuted prior to 1671, but those unlucky enough to be apprehended thereafter faced an increasingly varied and drastic series of punishments, especially in the eighteenth and nineteenth centuries. The 1671 Act imposed a fine of twenty shillings or three months' imprisonment for each hare killed, with further provision to confiscate dogs, nets and other 'engines' found in the possession of the unqualified. In 1707 this was raised to a £5 blanket fine, or imprisonment for three months. And in 1711 the penalty for possessing a snare, greyhound or dead hare – offences that did not necessarily involve hunting – was made equal with the actual taking of game. In the latter half of the eighteenth century, when organized poaching was perceived as a serious threat to the social order, these punishments escalated, beginning with a 1770 act which made imprisonment and public whipping mandatory for all night poachers. This was repealed three years later with fines of between £10 and £50 (huge sums) depending

on previous convictions, with those convicted of two or more offences liable to up to twelve months' imprisonment plus public whipping. As if this wasn't severe enough, the notorious Night Poaching Act of 1800 made provision for 'gangs' of poachers – actually two or more persons – to be punished under the Vagrant Act and pressed into the army or navy, or sent to prison at hard labour for up to two years. Two further acts tightened the screw still further, partly in response to the fact that the punishments for illegally taking even a hare were now so severe that resistance to apprehension by gamekeepers was common. In 1817 any poacher found with firearms, bludgeons or other 'offensive weapons' could be transported for seven years; in 1828 between seven and fourteen years' transportation was prescribed for offenders apprehended in the company of two or more persons if any one of the three was armed. There was an extraordinary rise of committals to prison for game offences in the second half of the eighteenth century, with numbers kept artificially low during the Napoleonic wars due to pressing. Carlyle may have thought that the French Revolution was made by the poachers of France, but Napoleon was defeated in part by the press-ganged poachers of England. As for the now seemingly drastic recourse to transportation, it's bitterly referred to as almost an inevitability in one of the best-known nineteenth-century poaching ballads, 'Van Diemen's Land', which exists in a score of variants in Britain, Ireland, Australia and North America:

> Come all you gallant poachers,
> That ramble void of care,
> That walk out on a moonlight night
> With your dog, your gun and snare.
> The harmless hare and pheasant
> You have at your command,

Francois Desportes, *Self-portrait as Huntsman*, 1699, oil on canvas.

Not thinking of your last career
Upon Van Diemen's land.[26]

Even before laws were instituted to press and transport game offenders (some 8,500 of whom were transported in the three years leading up to the earliest version of this ballad, from 1830) there is evidence that influence was exerted upon Justices of the Peace by the land-owning gentry to rid the land of what were perceived by some as two-legged vermin. A letter written in the 1770s from a land-owner to a local justice of the peace declares that 'one of the Burton brothers has declar'd that in spite of me he will kill a hare when he can', and goes on to ask 'would not a recommendation from You to the Captain of the Press Gang at Hull, put those young men in a way of becoming usefull subjects?'[27] The author of *A Dialogue . . . Upon the Subject of the Game Laws Relative to Hares, Partridges and Pheasants*, published in the following year, was convinced that recourse to such laws resulted in 50 prosecutions 'commenced upon tyrannical and revengeful principles' for every one 'founded upon the honourable notion of serving the publick'.[28]

The ideology which constructed formalized hare hunting as a noble, health-giving, superlative sport involved a reverse side which construed poaching as essentially vicious, over and above the otherwise tautological observation that it was a criminal act. To country gents the primary characteristic of a poacher was that he was not a sportsman. If labourers, apprentices and other 'men of small worth' were allowed to hunt game, they would soon begin to neglect their trades and, shortly thereafter, lose all sense of morality. And even as late as the monograph on the hare in the still collected and read *Fur and Feather* series (a book put together by a retired colonel, an Anglican vicar and 'The Hon. Gerald Lascelles') the Reverend H. A. MacPherson cannot refrain from referring to hare poachers as inveterate blackguards, for whom public whipping would be good medicine. Or as he puts it, 'there are plenty of idle rascals in the world for whom the judicious application of a well-furnished birch is fine physic'.[29] This was in 1896. Earlier in the century no poaching crime involving hares was considered too small, and no punishment for poaching too severe. In 1829 a fourteen-year-old girl, Jane Vickers, was sent to prison at hard labour for three months for merely picking up a hare from a snare set by her father. In 1826, in a notorious case, a man was hanged for wounding a gamekeeper in a poaching 'affray'.[30] A sufficient sense of the perceived injustice of such laws and punishments can be got from the fact that William Cobbett declared in an 'Open Letter to Peel' that if he was allowed to begin setting the country to rights, 'the *first thing*, the *very first* would be to *repeal the law for the transporting of poachers*'.[31]

A *Punch* cartoon, with the caption *'Sport!' or, A Battue Made Easy*, 1845.

The Reverend MacPherson also complains of Lloyd George's Ground Game Act of 1880, and it is worth pointing out that before this act even tenant farmers were not legally allowed to shoot or otherwise harm hares on their land. And this during periods when they were hardly scarce. Mary Cresswell, a maverick tenant farmer who was eventually to voluntarily transport herself to America where she wrote *Eighteen Years on Sandringham Estate* writes of there being so many 'preserved' hares on her rented land that they would 'snowball' after being started, and run before her pony like a pack of hounds.[32] They may have been naturally abundant in Norfolk, but not sufficiently so for the Prince Consort, who supplemented stocks for shooting by importing them from Europe. The husband of Victoria was at the forefront of the fashion for the grand 'battue', in which game was shot in increasingly grotesque numbers. *Punch* ridiculed such sport in a cartoon of 1845 (*Sport! or, A Battue Made Easy*)

John Leech cartoon, *The Game Laws; or, the Sacrifice of the Peasant to the Hare,* from *Punch*, 1846.

which shows Albert, seated in a drawing room, letting off both barrels at a pheasant while two hares take cover behind the furniture and a third lies shot, just as it was to pillory the game laws with a Leech cartoon of 1846, self-explanatorily entitled *The Game Laws; or, The Sacrifice of the Peasant to the Hare*. 'Who owns the hare that runs over the lea?' asks the popular nineteenth-century ballad, 'Who Owns the Game?', and the answer was still the land-owning classes. In the decades leading up to the committal to prison of Jane Vickers for picking up a single hare, the development of breech-loading guns and the increasing popularity of battues led to an escalation in numbers of hares killed undreamed of by former generations of hunting gentry. In 1796 the Duke of Bedford and six others killed 80 pheasants and 40 hares in a few hours. In 1810 the same number of guns accounted for 107 pheasants and 100 hares in the course of a day's shooting. In 1849 3,000 hares were killed on a Norfolk estate between Monday morning and Saturday night; 2,442 in the 1894 season on an estate in Newmarket.

The social status of hare coursing in England was eventually complicated by the fact that, with the gradual erosion of the game laws, it became as much a popular northern working-class pursuit as a gentrified one, generating in fact the idea that in hare hunting 'social extremes meet'. Queen Victoria may have summoned to her presence a greyhound so distinguished that it won the Waterloo Cup twice, and the father of the present Queen of England died after a morning spent bagging a few hares at Sandringham, but the word 'coursing' is now as likely to bring with it images of flat caps, whippets and lurchers as of its original aristocratic, landowning and even regal status. Just as the widespread practice of 'illegal' coursing – illegal even before the recent ban, since it takes place on farmland without the permission of the farmer – is associated in England with motley assortments of long-dogs, some stolen for purpose, spilling out of the back of unmarked travellers' vans. The same cannot be said for hunting with packs, for some of the last to be in operation in England were kept at military officer-training academies (including Sandhurst); by public schools (including Eton); and by Oxbridge colleges.

The long history of hare hunting has been paralleled by a history of thinking about it in relation to wider issues concerning cruelty to animals, with hares tending to focus feelings of ambivalence about hunting, as well as outright revulsion. Political distaste for and protest against game law was by no means always combined with a revulsion against hare hunting itself, most obviously not for those who wished to merely extend

A late 19th-century German target with three hares motif.

the franchise so that anyone wishing to do so could hunt. Cobbett was an enthusiastic hare hunter as well as a scourge of the laws that regulated it. On the other hand there have been hunting enthusiasts who have worried over the moral legitimacy of killing hares, at least from the time of Arrian. Gascoigne is a classic case in point: running with the hounds in his prose, then holding with the hare in the poem which is appended to it. Gascoigne's poem begins and ends unequivocally: 'Are mindes of men, become so voyde of sense,/ That they can joye to hurte a harmlesse thing? . . . Some sporte perhaps: yet Grevous is the glee/ Which endes in Bloud, that lesson learne of me.'[33]

In Shakespeare's 'Venus and Adonis' the goddess's coded attempt to persuade Adonis to hunt hare rather than boar is similarly undermined by sympathy for the quarry, in a five-stanza detour describing an actual hare hunt:

> Then shalt thou see the dew-bedabbled wretch
> Turn, and return, indenting with the way;
> Each envious briar his weary legs doth scratch,
> Each shadow makes him stop, each murmur stay:
> For misery is trodden on by many,
> And being low never reliev'd by any.[34]

The phrase 'dew-bedabbled' is lifted from a contemporary translation of Montaigne's essay 'On Cruelty', and the poem turns the hunted hare into an image of 'inhuman' humanity, tyrannizing over the weakest. Montaigne's influential essay builds upon Pythagorean and Christian attitudes towards animals to construct a critique of hunting, but is motivated by a personal aversion to seeing even a chicken's neck pulled, or to hearing the scream of a 'seely dew-bedabbled hare . . . when she is seized upon by hounds'. And this despite the fact that (in the very same sentence) 'hunting is a very great pleasure to me'.[35] Shakespeare's persecuted hare runs in the mainstream of humanist aversion to and critique of hunting. In Sir Thomas More's *Utopia* it is seen as a lowly form of butchery rather than as an ennobling art. His Utopians not only took no pleasure in hunting but failed to understand the pleasure derived from it by others. For More it made as much sense to watch a dog chasing another dog as to watch one coursing a hare, and he composed a Latin epigram in which a hare thrown to the hounds cries out to protest its 'innocence'.[36]

Attacks on cruel sports that were aristocratic and implicated in the game laws naturally encoded or implied wider social protest. In England there is also a specifically Christian vein of protest against hare hunting. Protestant attacks on cruel recreations, as Keith Thomas has pointed out, goes back at least to the mid 1500s. Before the Civil War dissenters concentrated their attacks on bear-baiting and cock-fighting, but subsequently widened their scope to include hare coursing. Writing in 1677, Edward Bury thought that 'to sport ourselves' in the death of hares 'seems cruel and bloody . . . suppose thou heardst such a poor creature giving up the ghost to speak in this manner . . . "Oh man, what have I done to thee? . . . I am thy fellow creature?"'[37]

No doubt such flagrant anthropomorphism cut little ice with committed hunters and apologists for hunting. In the seventeenth century Bulstrode Whitelocke held that hunting did nothing to make hares or deer unhappier than they would have been anyway. An opinion, incidentally, which was still being used by hare hunting lobbyists in the run-up to its recent ban, though one not supported by the scientific evidence used by Parliament to justify it. Seventeenth- and eighteenth-century discourse on hare hunting tended to emphasize both the 'harmlessness' of hares and, as did the earlier humanists, the connection between killing them for sport and a coarsening of the conscience leading to greater cruelties. In 1776 Francis Mundy denounced hare hunters as nothing less than a 'murderous crew', who 'in harmless blood their hands imbue', and in 1788 we can find it still being rhetorically allied to even more dubious sporting pursuits, and described as no more or less 'inhuman and barbarous' than bull-baiting.[38]

In one of the most renowned of all anti-hunting poems, 'The Hunting of The Hare' by the seventeenth-century writer Margaret Cavendish, a description of a hare hunt in emotive detail leads to a conclusion which has 'Man', and not just the hare-hunters 'Making their Stomacks, Graves'. For Cavendish this particular quarry becomes an apt vehicle for upping the stakes and challenging the idea that 'Nature' was God-given for men 'to Tyrranize upon'.[39] In Alexander Pope's 'Windsor Forest' a vignette of a hare pursued by beagles is used to wittily reverse the usual argument from nature in defence of hunting ('Beasts, urg'd by us, their fellow beasts pursue,/ And learn of man each other to undo'),[40] in a poem which also undermines the sanguinary association between hunting and war by linking 'the mazes of the circling hare' to 'th'amazed, defenceless' citizens of a besieged city.[41] Pope links his human and animal quarry in a play on 'amaz'd' and the 'mazes' of the hare. Another eighteenth-century poet, William Somervile, in his long poem *The Chase*, focuses upon this aspect of the hare's escape strategy when hunted (leaving the chasing pack to 'unravel wile by wile/ Maze within maze')[42] but to very different ends. Somervile does so not only in order to construct the hare as an admirable and worthy adversary, a common enough strategy of hunters, but to suggest in a curious passage that its behaviour shows evidence of God-given reason:

Samuel Howitt (1765–1822), an etching depicting a coursed hare.

Let cavillers deny
that brutes have reason; sure 'tis something more,
'Tis heav'n directs, and strategems inspires
Beyond the short extent of human thought.

Curious, that is, inasmuch as it reverses the usual Christian justification for the treatment of 'lower', by definition 'unreasonable' creatures, only to then suggest that this 'thinking' animal has been created for the express purpose of providing pleasure for the hunters.

Somervile no doubt writes with a period awareness of objections to hare hunting which were part of a general change in sensibility with regard to animals. As do Addison and Steele when they give an account of their fictional Sir Roger de Coverley sparing a hare he has hunted and keeping it instead as a pet. The poet William Cowper's prose account of his own keeping of several hares as pets was much read and admired.[43] James

Thomson, in a passage in his *The Seasons*, can stand here to illustrate a wholesale reversal of the traditional apologies for the 'nobility' of hare hunting, construing it as a survival of barbarism rather than an exquisite art:

> Upbraid, ye ravening tribes, our wanton rage
> For hunger kindles you, and lawless want;
> But lavish fed, in Nature's bounty rolled,
> To joy at anguish, and delight in blood,
> Is what your horrid bosoms never knew.
> Poor is the triumph o'er the timid hare![44]

The very reason used to distinguish it as 'sport' – the fact that it was not undertaken as a source of food – becomes for Thomson a sign of its decadence. The frequency with which such poetic anti-hunting sentiments were focused upon the hare is remarkable.

In his long poem *Rural Sports* John Gay includes a heavily ironized encomium on hare hunting, ending with the hounds tearing 'with gory mouth the screaming prey', and the sharply disingenuous exclamation: 'What various sport does rural life afford!'[45] By the time of Richard Jago's long poem *Edge-Hill, or, the Rural Prospect Delineated and Moralized*, in 1767, a side-swipe at the hare-hunters has become almost conventional, along with the construction of the hare as an archetypal 'innocent' victim. Jago's hare is a 'poor, trembling wretch . . . Guiltless of blood, and impotent of wrong'.[46] Even eighteenth-century novelists such as Henry Fielding could not mention the animal without reflecting on the cruelty of hunting it, upon its place in the moral as well as actual landscape. William Blake's couplet in his visionary poem 'Auguries of Innocence', 'Each outcry of the hunted Hare/ A fibre from the Brain doth tear',[47] provides, in brilliantly compressed form, a kind of epitome of this line of literary protest. It proposes a human–animal relationship that is both visceral and moral, with the word 'fibre' aptly chosen to give a sense of weirdly physical connectedness between human and hare, while at the same time suggesting the phrase 'moral fibre'. It thus stands on its head the traditional notion that hare hunting could promote the kind of benefits outlined by Xenophon, proposing rather that cruelty in the relatively minor case of hunting a hare for sport does significant damage to right thinking and conduct in their entirety, while at the same time contesting the Cartesian idea that animals were machine-like, lacking the capacity to properly experience pain. It was only left for Robert Burns to bring such poetic protests fully into the era of hunting with firearms. His 'The Wounded Hare' begins with a curse on whoever shot it, and in conclusion ratchets up the pathos by wondering whether it might have been a nursing mother with leverets that are now sure to die.[48]

Blake's vocalizing hare combines the notion of political 'outcry' or protest with the fact that, though otherwise silent, hares

Three leverets found next to their dead mother, Somerset, England, 2003

will scream when caught by dogs or natural predators. This vocalization has been traditionally likened to the cry of a human infant (Bewick's hunted hare 'screamed . . . like a child')[49] including by recent hunters and poachers. It was also noted as early as the eighteenth century that this made the hare an especially suitable vehicle for sympathy, and for protesting blood-sports.[50] Though it was also suitable because of its 'innocence' or innocuous character (the arguments used to justify the hunting of the predatory fox did not apply), and because of its widely testified to intelligence; as well as for the fact that it was politically implicated in game law, and that aristocratic hunting had virtually removed another basic justification for hunting, namely, the taking of animals for food. Fast-forwarding to the present day: before the recent ban on hunting hares with dogs was put into effect in England and Wales, the Hare Hunting Association submitted a document which specifically addressed the emotive issue of hares vocalizing *in extremis*. They do so it was argued – though without evidence and unconvincingly – not in agony or extreme distress but as an automatic reaction to being 'held', and as a warning signal to other hares. Far from being a sound that should trigger any sympathy in us, we should think of it as one which is, so to speak, strictly between hares.[51]

At the beginning of the nineteenth century *The Hare, or, Hunting Incompatible with Humanity, Written as a Stimulus to Youth Towards a Proper Treatment of Animals* gives a rather different 'voice' to a hare which is well-versed in the sentiments of its sympathizers: 'I had yet to learn, that though one of the most innocent, yet I was the most persecuted of animals – though one of the most defenceless, yet there was as much strength and malice exercised against me as against the strongest.'[52] This heavily didactic prose fiction, which seems expressly designed to follow Locke's dictum that literature for children should

Hare turned hunter, from *Struwwelpeter, or, Pretty Stories and Funny Pictures*, 1845, by Heinrich Hoffmann.

contribute to their being 'bred up in an abhorrence of killing and tormenting any living creature', goes on to put its hare-narrator through a series of misadventures – including capture and use for coursing – before finding refuge and a happy ending with a kindly protector. An example of the hare's contribution to the animalization of children's literature, it is also prototypical of

Hare sitting in a field.

countless subsequent animal stories and films for children, down to the era of Disney and beyond. When in *Hard Times* Dickens wittily describes the Gradgrind children as being 'coursed' in the classroom of M'Choakumchild, 'like little hares', he was relying on both Victorian liberal aversion to actual bloodsports and an association between childhood and lagomorph 'innocence'.[53]

In the twentieth century pro-hunt lobbyists have frequent recourse to the phrase 'Bambi effect' to refer to a perceived sentimental and anthropomorphizing element in outraged reactions to bloodsports. The phrase might have easily become 'Hare effect', or 'Friend Hare effect', for in Felix Salten's novel, *Bambi,* it is Friend Hare (cutely converted into a rabbit in the Disney film) and other lepuses that provide the focus for some its more extreme pathos. The children's classic *Struwwelpeter,* by Heinrich Hoffmann, though produced from a diametrically opposite desire to divest their literature of overtly didactic purposes, nevertheless includes the narrative of a huntsman who is bested – disarmed and hunted in turn – by a hare: a version of that motif which is to be found in medieval and Renaissance imagery, as

Postcard, Canada 1910: 'When we go after anything we get it.'

Greyhound with trophy in the form of a mounted hare's head, 1924.

well as in Hugo's *Les Misérables,* where it is used as an example of a politically charged imaginary 'revenge' devised by an actually powerless peasantry. In Hoffmann it's a pure example of a 'tricksterish' prey species outwitting a predator, of the kind which children find so satisfying, and the hare-as-trickster motif is reprised in the Bre'r Rabbit stories. For the original protagonist of these stories is by common consent thought to be a hare rather than a rabbit, translocated from its place in African folk tales.

Lewis Carroll's work was hugely influential in diverting the course of children's literature away from stodgy didacticism. The leporids in his most famous work are playfully morphed upon a traditional contrast which would have made sense to Kropotkin: the White Rabbit a fussy courtier obsessed with time; the March Hare all crazily laid-back insouciance. But Carroll was also a committed anti-vivisectionist and opponent of hunting – the latter concern finding its way into his novel for children, *Sylvie and Bruno* (1889), both in an explicit preface

Hare coursing at the 157th Waterloo Cup, Lancashire, England.

which refers to his 'deep wonder and sorrow' with regard to hunting, and in the narrative itself which includes an incident in which the young Sylvie comes across a hare which has been hunted by harriers and died 'of fright and exhaustion'. The narrator must then explain to a shocked and inquiring Sylvie why men hunt, getting into difficulty by placing its origins with the necessary extermination of fierce creatures. 'Are hares fierce?', asks Sylvie.

> 'No', I said. 'A hare is a sweet, gentle, timid animal – almost as gentle as a lamb.' 'But if men *love* hares, why – why –' her voice quivered, and her sweet eyes were brimming over with tears. 'I'm afraid they *don't* love them, dear child.' 'All children love them', Sylvie said. 'All *ladies* love them.' 'I'm afraid even *ladies* go to hunt them sometimes.'[54]

With this distinctly Victorian sentimental scene we are a world away from hare hunting as good training for war; from the hare as the most marvellous beast of the feudal chase; from legislation for and agitation against its status as 'game'. As well as from the Fritz Freleng cartoon, *Hare Meets Herr* (1945), in which Bugs Bunny (clearly a leporine) makes hay with Hitler and Goebbels in the Black Forest after taking a wrong turn in Albuquerque. But still in the direct line of those cultural constructions of the hare having to do with its historical status as specifically human quarry. In the twentieth century such anti-coursing writers as Henry Salt could draw upon what amounts to a historically deep structure of feeling regarding the hare, as could, including up to the present day in Ireland, more pragmatic and campaigning anti-bloodsports groups. Even modern greyhound racing owes its existence to such feeling, for the inventor of the mechanical hare was motivated by a desire to prevent the use of live quarry. Newspaper reporting of the last Waterloo Cup depicted an almost carnivalesque culmination to what has been historically at stake in hare hunting and coursing, with battle lines drawn up between a crowd consisting of

Hare coursing at Newmarket, England, 2000.

on the one hand 'toffs and chavs' and on the other outraged enclaves of 'antis'. A Martin Rowson cartoon used in one such newspaper provides an appropriate image with which to end: a bloodied hare linking arms with a ruddy countryman and hunt protestor, in a rendition of 'Auld Lang Syne'.

4 Painted and Plastic Hare

To hunt the hare as both subject and sign through the long history of its visual representation is to find it in positions of perhaps surprising prominence as well as intriguing marginality. The coursed hare placed prominently in Pisanello's *Vision of St Eustace* provides an early example of an attempt to depict the animal naturalistically, and of the visual allure for painters of its form. His rendering of the hound-hare figure was singled out for particular praise by contemporaries, and it does beautifully capture the physical homology or visual rhyme between pursuer and pursued (in Russian the graceful tapering of the hound from chest to hips is known as 'the hare-bend'), with the hare exceeding even such late fourteenth-century 'copy-book' drawings as the one by Giovanni de' Grassi which shows a running hare on a page with a roebuck, a wolf and a leopard – an exercise in comparative form with no regard to scale. Beneath Pisanello's hound-hare figure, however, there is a blank scroll, placed there in allusion to the fact that this is an image to be read. In the legend of St Eustace a vision of Christ crucified appeared between the antlers of a hunted stag. The subsequent conversion of this Roman soldier to Christianity tropes the idea of the hunter hunted. Pisanello's hound and hare echo and reinforce the idea: the crucified Christ is 'like' the hunted hare, but also like the hound in his role as a 'hunter of souls'.

16
capriolo
Lepore
uolpe
Leonpardo

Hare and hound from *The Vision of St Eustace* by Pisanello, 1436, egg tempera on poplar.

Roebuck, hare, wolf and leopard, in a depiction by Giovanni de Grassi designed to be used as a stock pattern for painters, c. 1389–98, pen and washes on parchment.

Pisanello's hare occurs as part of a fusion between the symbolic and even mystical valences of animals and an observation and endorsement of them in their own right and specificity. It is unlike in this respect such non-naturalistic, crazily cryptic, roughly contemporary marginal images as the one which depicts

Hares hunting men: the world turned upside down in the margin of a romance of Alexander the Great in French verse, 1344.

a hybrid man/snail ridden by a hare fighting a dog astride a hare, and the one which has an anthropomorphized hare (looking like a person in a pantomime hare suit) pursuing a hunter at bay at the top of a tree, then carrying him slung over its shoulder on a pole. The theme of the hare turned hunter occurs frequently in images of 'the world turned upside down' in illuminated manuscripts. It was also treated in a lost canvas by Cranach, appears in a detail of Bosch's *Garden of Earthly Delights* (1503–4) – and is to be found most elaborately and wittily in Virgil Solis's *Hares Roasting a Hunter*.

If the traditionally 'timid' or even cowardly hare provides a peculiarly apt vehicle for such cartoonish, carnivaleque reversals, it could also be used subtly in a painting such as Uccello's monumental *The Rout of San Romano* (1450–56). Three hares can be seen in the background of the panel showing Bernardino della Ciarda being struck off his horse. Two are fleeing across cultivated fields from a sight-hound working with crossbowmen, while the third seems to be running confused in the direction of the dog. Della Ciarda was the commander of the Sienese mercenary army; his ambush of a smaller Florentine force is commemorated in the painting, and Uccello's hares in panicked flight echo the rout of della Ciarda's forces in unflattering terms, and in a manner designed to please the painter's Florentine patron. A particular satisfaction at the downfall of della Ciarda can be easily surmised since he had previously fought for the Florentines. Hence, perhaps, given this additional source of animus against him, the coded ascription to the defeated of 'hare-heartedness'. Shakespeare could use the phrases 'coward hares' and 'hare-hearted' in military contexts, and in a famous speech have Henry v of England convert the French to coursed hares ('the game's afoot')[1] while the English troops strained in the slips. Even Byron could revert to the tradition by describing Napoleon as 'a lion in the conquering hour/ In wild defeat a hare'.[2]

Compared to Pisanello's hare, Uccello's are rudimentary if lively outlines, due to their position in the painting but also to their function as ciphers. In Titian's *The Worship of Venus* a hare is given a position at the centre of the canvas, conscripted there for its rather different symbolic association with the titular goddess and painted with detailed and lively naturalism. That Titian was no stranger to the uses of lagomorph and hunting symbolism is evident from an earlier canvas, the so-called *Sacred and Profane Love* in the Galleria Borghese, Rome. In *The Worship*

Virgil Solis, *Hares Roasting a Hunter*, 16th century, engraving.

A hare mobbed by cherubs in Titian's *The Worship of Venus*, 1518–20, oil on canvas.

of Venus a large group of riotous chubby cupids is depicted eating fruit, dancing, wrestling, kissing and embracing. The hare which has been chased and caught at the centre of this group reflects classical precedents, and has been converted by Titian into a cipher for playful, unlicensed eroticism. At the same time it has been painted both wittily and naturalistically to convey the animal's nervousness at being thus mobbed, in such a way as to suggest that if not held as it is by one of the cupids, it would take the opportunity to leap out of the realm of the symbolic into which it has been conscripted.

A roughly contemporary image from 1511, a woodcut depicting Adam and Eve by the Lutheran pupil of Albrecht Dürer, Hans Baldung Grien, provides a stark contrast with Titian's painting, and an illustration of how the hare was used to signify an opposite take on sexuality: a fundamentalist's association of it with the very origin of sinfulness, and with the fallen state of the world. Baldung Grien's hares are depicted at the foot of the tree from which Eve has plucked an apple, and to which the text '*Lapsus Humani Generis*' (The Fall of Mankind) is attached. His image, with its Adam fondling the apple-like breast of Eve, proposes the advent of carnality as the source of that *lapsus*. One of the lepuses is depicted side-on, the other from behind, suggesting a posture of sexual receptiveness. As well as clearly signalling the 'fall' into lustful carnality, the presence of these hares also recalls a consequence of that fall: the necessity to procure food by spilling blood in the hunt. Baldung Grien's hares are not taken from life, they are flatly cartoonish ciphers clearly cribbed from the one in Dürer's own *Adam and Eve* (1504). And it is in the work of Dürer that there is to be found the single most remarkable lagomorph in painting. Plagiarized and copied in the sixteenth century, and massively reproduced in the age of mechanical reproduction, his 1502 watercolour of a hare is both an innovative and unsurpassed epitome of northern Renaissance verisimilitude and a work with an intriguing afterlife.

The first thing that strikes any viewer of the image is its exceptional lifelikeness. Dürer seems to have painted every hair in his subject's fur ('one could swear', according to Panofsky, 'that there is not a single hair missing')[3] but also to have combined the detail with superb modelling and colouring. The detail contributes to but does not distract from an overall ability to convey the animal's living presence, its 'hareness', so to speak. This is aided by two innovations so taken for granted as to be invisible to a modern viewer. Before Dürer, animals generally – and hares invariably – were drawn side-on. And the *Young Hare* is probably the first example of a wild animal drawn from a live, probably tame, specimen sitting before the artist in his studio. Looked at closely, we can make out the transom and mullion of a window reflected in the hare's eye. The latter detail an innovation so radical, incidentally, that it seems hardly to have been understood even by painters who painstakingly copied and adapted the work. Hans Hoffmann, for instance, painted several works clearly cribbed from Dürer's hare, including two in which the animal is transposed to an exterior setting. And yet his *Hare Among Flowers* (1582) not only fails to omit the studio window reflected in its eye, a detail which makes no sense in the open-air setting, but actually exaggerates it.

Dürer's hare represents a kind of quantum leap forward in the depiction of animals, the equivalent in visual art of the rejection of 'authority' in natural history in favour of close first-hand observation. It was one of the first results of a period in Dürer's life when, dissatisfied with his work to date, he set about systematically studying perspective, human proportion and the proportions of animals. Dürer was also one of the first artists to use watercolour, and has worked the optical effect of rendering the texture of the fur by establishing its colours with a broad brush and then building up several layers of detailed, fine brushstrokes. He was also the first to pay visual attention to the animal's several distinct types of hair. There is further artfulness in the angle chosen from which to view the hare: exactly the right angle from which to give a sense of the power of its huge haunches in repose. Its sentience has been conveyed by the

Albrecht Dürer, *Young Hare*, watercolour and gouache on paper, 1502.

attention paid not just to its eye but to its whiskers and other facial vibrissae, as well as by slightly exaggerating the length of its ears in relation to the size of its skull, and the extent to which its right ear is alertly open. With its conveyance of the animal's sentience, power, gentleness and composure we might be tempted to speak of an unsurpassed rendering of its 'personality' as much as of its literal appearance, and the detail of the eye might even be read as an attempt to ascribe to the animal something like a sensitive soul, or at least a degree of subjectivity. The window shape in the eye is a classical topos or recurring device that Dürer introduced into German art for the first time in his self-portrait of 1500, and is a figure for the 'window of the soul' in addition to being a hyper-realistic detail.[4] It is, then, as if the hare is being credited with the ability to gaze inwards as well as about itself. With Dürer's hyper-realistic and curiously dignified depiction, at any rate, we are a world away from both the emblematic reduction of the animal to a figure for human 'lust' or cowardice, and its naturalistic place in hunting scenes.

Dürer himself was hardly unaware of the symbolic and iconic connotations of the animal. He refers to them in two other works. His *Holy Family with Three Hares* (1497) utilizes the connection in Christian iconography between the animal and the motherhood of Mary, while the number three probably also evokes the Trinity. In his *Adam and Eve* there are four animals including a cat and a hare between the feet of the two central human figures. These Dürer hares are utterly unlike the *Young Hare*, for the first three – playful leverets – are rudimentary to a degree not just in keeping with the formal constraints of the woodcut. Their cartoonish depiction seems designed to signify that they are being used emblematically. In *Adam and Eve* the hare is rendered more realistically, with more detail, partly in order to contrast the texture of its fur with the skin of Eve with which it is almost in contact, thus subtly reinforcing the sexually charged nature of the image.

The half a dozen or so extant sixteenth-century imitations of the *Young Hare* are notably inferior versions which serve to show Dürer's mastery and what happens with a return to copying a pre-existing image rather than the thing itself, though they also attest to the immediate popularity of the image amongst painters and patrons. One of the most interesting, designed as an illustration for a work of natural history, includes a version of the *Young Hare* in a scene with another similar hare, a squirrel, and a horned hare – the inclusion of the latter graphically underscoring a movement away from direct observation and back to copy-book 'authority'. One of the most mysterious places a version of Dürer's hare in the corner of a painting of St John on Patmos, along with a hare's skull,[5] the latter connecting it with the inclusion of hares as *memento mori* in still-life painting.

In the twentieth century Dürer's hare became one of the most mechanically reproduced and commodified images of an animal from the fine art tradition. There is a striking reflection on this phenomenon in a photograph by Angela Meier of a series of art books open at the page containing the *Young Hare*, showing how each reproduction varies slightly in colour from the others, in a visual equivalent of a Chinese-whisper effect.[6] Its general reproduction and dissemination has been so widespread that one recent art historian has seen it as contributing to nothing less than the 'bourgeois democratisation' of art, a contemptuous phrase in his handling of it, since the work has appealed to those 'for whom the word "art" has little meaning'.[7] It is worth noting here that its popularity must have as much to do with a liking for its subject as for any 'bourgeois' demand for hyper-realism in art, for there are other animal and plant studies by Dürer that are as superbly accomplished but have not achieved such currency.

Its universal appeal has also contended intriguingly with a tendency to construct it as a specifically German work. There is a classic illustration of this tendency in the work of Wölfflin, in a passage which moves seamlessly from describing its superlatively 'textural qualities' to asserting that 'a strong feeling for texture' is one of the main characteristics of German art. Further still, to contrast the birth and development of still-life painting in 'the north' of Europe with 'southern' painters' suspicion of the genre as 'a mere trick of illusion'.[8] Though this hardly stands up as even generalizing art history, it is fascinating to see how it prepared the ground for the hijacking of Dürer's work during the Third Reich, where the *Young Hare* was issued in the series of 'Reichsdruckerei' – prints designed to find their way into every good German home – becoming, as one recent writer has it, 'prey to hyper-German kitschiness'.[9] Dürer's work was co-opted by the Nazis as an epitome of figurative art, a high-point from which to berate 'degenerate' modernism. Joseph Beuys's work has its roots in a coming to terms with the aftermath of the Second World War, including in a confrontation with and reworking of Teutonic culture. No accident, then, that his fascination with the hare (a quintessential prey species taken as a totem animal in opposition to the Nazi use of the eagle as emblem) resulted in a series of works which did not fail to include his own *Young Hare*, a watercolour of a leveret which consists of little more than a pale lemon wash within a rudimentary outline, emphasizing the new-born fragility of an actual leveret rather than the sentience and power of Dürer's (not conspicuously 'young') hare. The post-war German artist Sigmar Polke has produced versions of Dürer's hare which allude to its commodification: a rudimentary outline placed on a wallpaper background; another in which the outline of the hare is made from a rubber band. In a work by Walter Schreiber the idea that Dürer's image has captured the essence of a wild animal is questioned and even mocked by combining multiple reproductions of it in wooden frames covered with chicken-wire and containing actual grass and vegetables. Its title, *Rabbit-hutch*, and the effect which it gives of eerily cloned and inappropriately confined animals also seems devised in allusion to the commodification of Dürer's watercolour, and to its art-historical use as almost a fetish of hyper-realism. Dieter Roth's more crudely irreverent *Shit Hare* (1975) was produced by filling a chocolate 'bunny' mould with excrement, in a gesture as sceptical of Beuys's shamanistic encounters with the hare as it is of the fetishization of Dürer's image.

Of the hundred or so animals depicted in Jacopo Bassano's sixteenth-century *The Animals Going into the Ark*, the hare is the only one running, and the only one without a mate, the first detail an allusion to its scatty dynamism, the second to its supposed hermaphroditism. But from the beginning of the seventeenth century onwards there is a plethora of conspicuously dead hares in oil painting: part of the flowering of the still-life tradition, with its sub-genres of market scene, kitchen scene and game piece. The earliest account of still-life painting is given by the Greek writer Philostratus in his *Imagenes*, and includes a description of a work depicting a live hare in a cage flanked by a dog and a second hare 'that hangs on the withered oak tree, his belly laid open and his skin stripped over the hind feet'. There are compelling reasons why the hare was a particularly alluring subject for later still-life painters. The French term for still-life is *nature morte*, and the genre is traditionally haunted by reminders of mortality. Due to its athletic vitality when living there are perhaps few things deader or 'stiller', so to speak, than a dead hare, its former fleetness underpinning meditations on the fleetingness of material existence. Due to its complex coat colour and multi-textured fur, the brown hare also provided painters with the opportunity, time and again, to effect a bravura contrast between it and some other surface (feathers, the carapace of a cooked lobster, pewter or porcelain vessels) and the animal's elongated form when hung as game provides a dramatic vertical dimension to otherwise horizontally determined scenes. One of the best accounts of the visual allure of the hare for such painters, and incidentally of its ambiguous status as fair game, comes not from the history of art but in an essay published in the 1880s by Richard Jefferies:

> Overtaken by the cartridge, still the hare, as he lies in the dewy grass, is handsome. Lift him up and his fur is full of

> colour, there are layers of tint, shadings of brown within it, one under the other, and the surface is exquisitely clean. The colours are not really bright, at least not separately, but, they are so clean and so clear that they give the impression of warmth and brightness. Even in the excitement of sport regret cannot but be felt at the sight of those few drops of blood about the mouth which indicate that all this beautiful workmanship must now cease to be. Had he escaped, the sportsman would not have been displeased.[10]

Due to its currency as a sexual symbol the hare could also be used in hybrid still-life and genre scenes to focus a conceptual pun between *carne* and carnality, or to evoke the double meaning of 'venery'; pleasures of the flesh as well as of the chase. The depiction of hares in such paintings is also more or less loaded with the animal's legal status as one of the principal game animals, making them a visual reinforcement of aristocratic privilege for their purchasers and patrons, or of *nouveau riche* aspiration. Until the formation of the Batavian Republic in 1795, the laws limiting the hunting of game to the nobility in the Netherlands were as strict as those in England.[11]

One of the earliest proto-still-life paintings to contain dead hares is Pieter Cornelisz van Ryck's *Kitchen Scene* of 1604, a work non-naturalistically overloaded with every kind of dead meat in various stages of preparation. To the left of the picture a young woman in a low-cut blouse holds a side of pork in one hand and a basket of dead birds in the other, with the lower part of the pork supported by the hand of a grotesquely aged woman. In the centre of the picture there is a boy playing with a young dog, and to the right a man biting into an apple with bared teeth and flanked on one side by a flayed carcass and on the other by hanging hares. There is a cat attempting to steal a string of sausages from the chair on which the arm of this figure rests and the head of a hound protruding into the picture next to the chair. It's a painting, then, that's also heavily overloaded with sexual (and *vanitas*) elements, with even the otherwise entire hare with its underside showing displaying a genital gash rather than the rip in its stomach which would facilitate the removal of its entrails. Though cruder than the still-lifes proper which were to be developed throughout the century, and to bring the hare into a central position, it is a painting worth noticing for the elements

Pieter Paul Rubens and Frans Snyders, *The Fig*, c. 1615, oil on canvas.

which it makes manifest, rendering in a raw form aspects which were to be increasingly latent, aestheticized and subtle.

The Flemish painter Frans Snyders (1579–1657) was one of the first to bring about this change. Snyders was a specialist animal painter who both contributed to and broke from the allegorical tradition in which he was schooled, including in a number of still-lifes in which hares figure centrally. In Rubens' erotically charged *The Fig*, Snyders contributed the array of dead game flanking the two human figures in a landscape – a woman in *décolleté* holding a basket of fruit including a fig which is being taken by the right hand of a huntsman, while his left hand holds a hawk the back of which is in contact with two hanging hares. The sexual symbolism is obvious, and the hares are even positioned to mirror human sexual congress, while a dog reaches up to steal one of the grapes hanging on a stalk from the basket.

Frans Snyders, *Fruit Piece with Small Game, a Lobster and a Blue Flagon*, c. 1605–10, oil on canvas.

With its dogs snarling over raw meat and woman offering fruit to a leering man while a dead hare hangs over the woman's shoulder on which the man's hand rests, Snyders's own *Seller of Game* reprises the themes of the Rubens and van Ryck paintings. But his early still-life painting proper was more subtle and sophisticated, and included a number of enigmatic arrangements of fruit and game, for example four paintings in each of which single hares are arranged on a table with a lobster and grapes, along with various other items.

These paintings were innovative inasmuch as they placed dead hares in central close-up on a kitchen table, their elements emerging dramatically from a dark background, the hares painted with great detail and showing minimal alteration to the form they have when living. With no obvious narrative element, everything takes place in a series of formal echoes and contrasts: the texture of the hares' fur contrasted with the shiny carapaces of the lobsters and with porcelain and brass plates and vessels; the highlight in the dead eye of the hare mirroring the highlights on the grapes; the ears and forepaws of the hares placed in formal relation to bunches of asparagus, and so on. These are paintings which effectively propose the visual beauty of the dead hare as an object of contemplation, and subject for the painter's skill in rendering it. But they are also paintings which play a subtle game of concealment and revelation with regard to the material and social origins and meaning of the arrangements depicted. Due to the game laws the hares are every bit as much 'luxury' items as the lobsters with which they are paired. The decision to paint the lobsters boiled might be seen as simply aesthetic – the rich red of their boiled state in preference to the matte bluish-black of the pre-boiled creature. But they have also thus been translated from the order of nature to the culture of the table, in contrast to the pre-cooked state of everything else in the paintings. And yet the rawness of the hares, their transitional status between living animal and dead meat, is decorously concealed. They bear no mark of the violence with which they must have been taken (and no sign of rigor mortis). In the two paintings in which the viewer might have otherwise seen the rips in their stomachs where their entrails were removed, Snyders has placed game birds on top of them to mask them from view. And in those paintings where the hares' heads are most prominent in the foreground of the picture, he has painted them with highlighted *living* eyes rather than glazed dead ones.

For the sake of an almost certainly aristocratic patron, then, Snyders has converted the food in these still-lifes into the realm of the aesthetic, erasing any trace of its provenance, let alone any sign of its implication, through the game laws, in a class struggle. His hares appear almost as willing victims, offering themselves up live like the creatures in certain English country house poems of the seventeenth century for which there was an equivalent genre in the Netherlands. And yet there is also evidence in these paintings of a subtle reintroduction of the violence which they work to exclude: in the red breast feathers of the birds which suggest the blood of the hares which they conceal; in the silver knife placed so that the blade seems to be disappearing into the back of a hare; even in the eerily sentient eyes which might read as meeting the viewer accusingly rather than willingly.

In the work of various painters of dead hares subsequent to Snyders there is an increasing emphasis upon mortality and violence; variations played upon their social and sexual significance and certain incorporations of them into what might be called metaphysical arrangements. In Willem van Aelst's *Fish, Lobster and Hare*, the lobster is so ripped as to be unrecognizable, and the central, elongated body of the hare is so arranged as to reveal a massive bloody gash in its stomach, its body contorted to

Willem van Aelst, *Fish, Lobster and Hare*, 1653, oil on canvas.

maximize the sense of violence. In Pieter Lindsay's *Dead Hare and Birds* (1663) the skull of a long-beaked bird with empty eye sockets parallels the dramatic vertical made by the dead-eyed hare hanging from one back leg. And, more generally in the various ways in which the hares are hung in these paintings, the hare assumes the role of quintessential victimhood over and above its simple status as naturalistically depicted dead game. This is most explicit in a much later Spanish painting, the *Kitchen Still-life* (1764) by Mariano Nani, in which an apparently live lamb in the foreground with its four legs trussed together is mirrored by a hare hanging directly above it from a game crown with its four legs identically trussed. In the work of Dutch and Flemish artists

working in the wake of Snyders, a centrally hanging hare is used in still-lifes constructed as theatres of violence. In Jan Fyt's *A Hare, Partridges and Fruit*, for instance, a heavy curtain has been partially withdrawn to reveal the scene, even though it is placed outside with neoclassical buildings in the background, as if to emphasize this theatricality. The outsize hare in this painting, bigger even than the dog in the foreground, is hanging from a rope attached to no obvious point of suspension, and is so positioned as to more resemble a deposition of Christ than a naturalistic game piece. Like the contorted hare which is as improbably nailed by one leg to a column in his *Still-life with Fruit, Dead Game and a Parrot*, it is also bloodily ripped. Fyt seems to have sought, between 1640 and 1660, ever more dramatic ways of positioning his hares, in order to manifest the violence which is glossed over in Snyders. In a third canvas (*Still-life of Game Birds and Hares with a Cat Nearby*) the violence inflicted on its intact and unmarked subjects has been siphoned into the crimson cloth or fallen curtain against which they are posed. But Fyt has rendered the viewing of the picture no less uncomfortable by hanging from a single back leg the central hare which seems to kick with its free one. It is an effect reproduced in his *Diana with her Hunting Dogs Beside the Kill*, in which an elaborate pile of dead game (including a swan, peacock, deer and wild boar) culminates in a hare swinging by one leg just out of reach of a dog which is craning to sniff it. This theatricality is developed in the work of a third artist who painted more than half a dozen still-lifes with hares, Jan Weenix. Weenix combines Fyt's spectacle of violence with Snyders's reticence about the kill. His hares are dramatically pinned, trussed, non-naturalistically suspended, but evince no other signs of corporeal violence, and are translated into highly aestheticized landscapes replete with neoclassical architectural details and statuary.

Jan Weenix, *Still-life with a Dead Hare*, 1682, oil on canvas.

In the work of two French painters of the late seventeenth and early eighteenth centuries the game-piece and still-life with hare was given a new direction. François Desportes and Jean-Baptiste Oudry were both celebrated *animaliers* catering to the taste for wildlife painting and court painters whose canvases celebrated hunting as an aristocratic pursuit and privilege. Desportes' flattering depictions of the aftermath of hunting rarely rise above a certain generic level and include hare motifs adopted from the Dutch and Flemish tradition and slightly vulgarized, such as the one in which a retriever is shown lapping blood from the gash in the stomach of an upturned hare posed above a pile of shot song- and game-birds: a celebration of the bloodthirstiness of hunting rather than any revelation of its ambivalence. In the more refined and resonant work of Oudry there is a series of game still-lifes which jettison all baroque clutter and context to focus on a pair of hanging animals sharing a single point of suspension; including a hare and a sheldrake, a hare and songbirds and, most spectacularly, a *Hare and a Leg of Lamb*. In this painting the dead but intact and seemingly even running hare (if tilted anti-clockwise through 180 degrees) is contrasted with a raw side of bloody meat, in a stark illustration of the passage from field to food.

Oudry's painting must have been well known to another, much finer French painter of the eighteenth century. According to his first biographer, Jean-Siméon Chardin's decision to become a painter of still-lifes occurred after he was gifted and depicted a dead hare,[12] and his numerous hare works complete the movement towards focused meditation present in Oudry's best work, and further away from the satisfying of wealthy patrons as practised by Desportes. The modernity of these paintings is best appreciated in contrast to their immediate art-historical context, for as one critic has put it, 'Chardin's prolonged meditation on brown crockery and the matted fur of dead hares took place in the midst of an efflorescence of luxury art – pink bodies, swirling fronds of gold ornament, rinsed allegorical skies: the Rococo style in all its Gallic glory.'[13] Gone is the clutter of the baroque game-piece with its piles of artfully arranged and combined dead animals and objects. Gone too the theatricality and

Jean-Baptiste Oudry, *Hare and a Leg of Lamb*, 1742, oil on canvas.

glamour, along with all mythological allusions and trappings. In his best hare paintings the animal has become the means for intense focus upon the earth-tones of its fur and the litheness of its form, painted in such a way as to exclude all but the most perfunctory reference to context and background. And yet this toning down and intensity of focus also becomes a means to re-introduce some of the traditional themes and resonances of the game still-life in a purer and subtler form.

Jean-Siméon Chardin, *Hare with Powder Flask and Game Bag*, 1728–30, oil on canvas.

That Chardin was capable of producing decorative and patron-pleasing post-hunt images in the style of Desportes and others is evidenced by *The Hound* (1724) and *The Water-Spaniel* (1730) though in both cases their quarry, a hare, takes centre stage away from the ostensible, titular subject. In his more characteristic and striking *Hare with Powder Flask and Game Bag*, Chardin uses the same hare in a starker, minimalist context posed against a simple scumbled brown wall, and whereas the lower half of its body is decorously concealed in the spaniel painting by the head and wing of a hanging duck, it is here shockingly exposed, legs splayed to reveal a bloody gash in its lower abdomen. The contorted position of its body, achieved by pinning one of its legs to the wall with a nail, is more reminiscent of a Crucifixion than a naturalistic larder scene, while the front half of its body, which seems about to slip off the shelf, echoes a deposition. Equally striking is the dynamic way in which Chardin has rendered the texture and colour of its fur and musculature. There is nothing remotely inert or object-like about the result. Here, rather, is a dead animal rendered in such a way as to make it seem livelier than most representations of living ones: to place it at an agonistic point between life and death.

Perhaps no wonder, then, that a recent critic has suggested a correlation between 'Chardin's fur' and the theories of his contemporary Julien Offray de La Mettrie, who argued for the recognition of a sensitive, material 'soul' in animals.[14] Be that as it may, in another hare painting executed around the same time – *Hare with Game Bag and Powder Flask* – he reprises the subject in a similarly dramatic manner. In relation to these two paintings it is worth noting that although Chardin also painted many still-lifes with dead rabbits the splayed, almost obscene posture was unique to his depiction of hares, possibly as some faint echo of the animal's reputation for 'lasciviousness'. If so, this would disrupt the universal perception of his work as peculiarly sexless. But it is more likely that this splaying has to do with the revelation of violence and mortality and with an aesthetic fascination with the litheness and anatomical form of the hare, since his earliest biographer suggests plausibly that he painted his first lagomorph because he 'found it beautiful'.[15] The second of the hares with game bag evinces a kind of rough beauty again hardly designed to cater for the collectors of decorative *retours de chasse*. The front half of the animal's body now lies prone, with its back turned to the viewer, with the length and softness of its horizontal ears emphasized in contrast to its splayed back legs: deathly repose contrasted as it were to the power-in-life of the heavily sinewed and muscled back legs which evoke both former movement and violation or indignity after death. In this painting Chardin does not fail to dispose traces of spilt blood, using red on an inner thigh to give even an intact and still furred leg a meaty quality, and placing blood on the stone ledge next to its nose and mouth. In both paintings a bluish cord or ribbon dissects the animal's genital area, and there is a kind of visual rhyme between its ears and the leather game bag, the latter a subtle allusion to the conversion of living animal to object for use.

In his, at first glance, more traditionally generic *A Soup Tureen with a Cat Stalking a Partridge and a Hare*, there is in play an equally subtle process of revelation and concealment, and an actually peculiar diversion from genre. As in many Dutch and Flemish game-pieces a bird is placed to partially obscure the hare precisely where an abdominal gash might be found, only to be reintroduced or suggested by the rash of red feathers against the white on the partridge's breast. This reticence is then countered by the gore dropping from the hare's swollen and protruding tongue and the blood on its ear. There is a further, most subtle suggestion of the idea of blood rather than of the substance itself in the red highlight in the silver soup tureen, with the open-mouthed, crouching and dwarfed cat serving as a conventional reminder of the raw animality that is the basis of even the most sophisticated cuisine. As in Chardin's other hare works, it is the centrally placed lagomorph – exaggerated in scale in relation to the cat – that dominates. In addition to its meditation upon mortality the canvas also invites a meditation upon nature and artifice, with the supremely artificial silverwork matched and outdone by the intricate musculature of the hare and the apparent minimalism of focus actually underpinned by a deliberate inclusion of a full range of elements: stone, metal, artefact, fruits, vegetables, living and dead animals.

It was Chardin's achievement in these paintings to invest his dead animals with pathos and gravitas whilst avoiding obvious

Jean-Siméon Chardin, *A Soup Tureen with a Cat Stalking a Partridge and a Hare*, 1727–28, oil on canvas.

sentiment, and to render his hares with such exactitude as to manifest their beauty without converting them into affectless objects for aesthetic contemplation. There are no nineteenth-century painted hares which remotely compare with these. Excepting, perhaps, Goya's stark image of a dead brace (*A Still-life of Dead Hares*), which was painted during the Napoleonic occupation of Spain, and which reflects obliquely upon the disasters of recent war. These hares have about them the air of executed and dumped human prisoners rather than of conventional subjects for a game-piece. The nineteenth century decline in the painted hare population, so to speak, was due partly to the decline of the still-life genre. And partly, one suspects, due to the demotion of the hare in a new hierarchy of 'interesting' animals as subjects for painting, as exemplified in the work of Delacroix and Landseer, with Landseer in particular preparing the ground for a subsequent embarrassment on the part of art historians with the very idea of 'animals in art'. On the one hand there is Delacroix's exotically stagey depiction of a hare being devoured by a lion, and the sculptor Antoine-Louis Barye's hare in the clutches of a panther (as if the animal's conventional European predators were not sufficiently dramatic as subjects); on the other the countless and for the most part undistinguished sporting prints of coursed and hunted hares. A surprising exception to this rule occurs in Turner's late painting *Rain, Steam and Speed* (1844), in which a running hare is dwarfed by a locomotive hurtling across a viaduct: a cipher of natural contrasted with mechanical velocity, with the hare also carrying the Romantically-inflected idea of the 'natural' world or environment being eclipsed by industrialism. But not until the beginning of the twentieth century is there another significant encounter between a centrally figured hare and major artist, in the work of Chaim Soutine.

In Soutine's work there is a rich vein of still-life painting which includes a number of sequences of studies of dead animals, including rays and other fish, various fowl, bovine carcasses and half a dozen canvases depicting hares. Soutine's animal still-lifes pay homage to a tradition which includes Rembrandt and Chardin, but also extend that tradition with their swirling, thickly encrusted, 'expressionistic' brushwork in which the violent death suffered by his subjects is matched by a kind of answering formal violence. Or by one in which, paradoxically, the paint takes on such an appearance of movement, animation and rough beauty as to transform its central, deathly, figurative element into an overall sense of pulsating vitality.

Soutine painted his hares in the early to mid-1920s, at a time when his visits to the Louvre to see works by Chardin and Rembrandt no doubt suggested the subjects for his beef and ray fish paintings. He was also shuttling between Paris and a studio in a farm building at Ceret, where he would have been in proximity with some of the actual subjects of his paintings. His general choice of subjects for the still-lifes has been scrutinized for its biographical, social and even religious significance. Despite his orthodox upbringing, Soutine almost invariably chose to paint non-kosher food, or animals in the process of becoming food. Having experienced great poverty and deprivation in his childhood and early manhood, his 'obsession' with food has been linked to the hunger that was a fact of life in the East European *shtetls* and linked further to the fact that, in adulthood, the stomach ulcers which eventually killed him prevented him from eating the kinds of food he depicted in his paintings, the subjects of which were thus under a kind of double prohibition. More intriguingly, and less reductively, we have his own account of a mundane early experience which he linked directly to his later development as a painter:

> Once I saw the village butcher slice the neck of a bird and drain the blood out of it. I wanted to cry out, but his joyful expression caught the sound in my throat. This cry, I always feel it there. When, as a child, I drew a crude portrait of my professor, I tried to rid myself of this cry, but in vain. When I painted the beef carcass it was still this cry that I wanted to liberate. I have still not succeeded.[16]

It is a remarkable passage in which this trapped cry – presumably of sympathy or horror – becomes associated with the very act of painting. Soutine's series of hares begins with a study of an eviscerated animal lying on its back on a table seen from above, legs splayed and chest cavity bloody, with a yellowish-white cloth between hare and table-top. The latter detail and unusual point of view add an element of anthropomorphism: we could be looking at a human figure lying racked by torture on a bed. The image is divested of all the usual accoutrements of kitchen still-lifes and game-pieces in an intense concentration upon the flayed flesh. In another of the earliest paintings in the series, *Hare with Forks*, a pair of outsize silver forks are anthropomorphized to give the impression of a pair of human hands tearing at the side of the prostrate animal. In both canvases the volume has been turned uncomfortably up on the disturbing element latent in all animal still-lifes. And what one post-war critic noted of Soutine's eviscerated cows and fowl – that they were open to be read as 'fetishistic reminders of man's darkest, cruellest, and most primitive instincts'[17] – can as readily be extended to them.

Though hardly less dramatic, something rather different occurs with the four paintings of hares which he did between 1925 and 1926. Each returns to the traditional verticality of the game still-life, with a single intact hare hanging head downwards, but with all naturalistic reference to food preparation or to any other context expunged, except for a stylized shutter which provides the background for one of them. *Hare Against Green Shutter* contains the at first sight most realistically depicted of Soutine's lepuses in its outline and colouring, with its reddish-buff and white fur highlighted against the deep greens and blacks of the painted shutter. Rotate the image right through 90 degrees, however, and the extent to which Soutine has stylized its posture is revealed. It is an image of a running or leaping hare, rather than of one subject to the usual laws of gravity. Combined with its skull-like death-grimace, it presents a striking variation upon the theme of *memento mori*, of the proximity of life and death.

In *Dead Hare* the hanging central figure is not so much defined against as on the point of merging with an abstract background, its body colour sharing some of its greens, blacks and yellows; its head skull-like and fur painted as if in the process of decay. In *Hare Against Blue Background* and *Hanging Hare* the process is taken further, with visibly decaying animals on the verge of losing their form and colour. The first, with face blackened to obliterate its features and the lower part of its body dislocated from the upper, contends against a void-like but still dynamic background. The second, the only one of his hares to hang entirely limp, is trussed with a tourniquet-like cord which has swollen its back-legs beyond recognition. Its grotesque head and upper body are about to be engulfed by one of the areas of pure black which are encroaching upon the thickly encrusted blues of the background.

In his painting *Landscape (The Hare)* (1927) Joan Miró's geometrically stylized hare is placed in relation to a huge spiral which alludes to the peculiar and intimate connection between *living* animal and environment, as does the title with its proposal of almost equivalence between its two main elements. In those paintings produced in the 1940s by Mark Rothko which

overleaf:
Left: Chaim Soutine, *Hare Against Green Shutter*, c. 1925–6, oil on canvas.

Right: Chaim Soutine, *Hare Against Blue Background*, c. 1924–5, oil on canvas.

hover on the border between figuration and abstraction, half a dozen use a stylized eagle-hare motif, sourced in the *Oresteia*, to reflect symbolically upon events in contemporary Europe. For Rothko this fused animal figure hovers to link Greek tragedy with the violence unleashed by Nazism.

In *Triptych Inspired by the Oresteia of Aeschylus* Francis Bacon devotes the left panel to a geometrically stylized hanging hare which is aborting through a mouth-like gash in its side, while a trail of blood seeps beneath an open door in the background. It alludes to the hares in still-life painting as well as to the omen in Aeschylus, omitting the eagles and warping image and theme with garish intensity. Hares figure most extensively and intriguingly, though, in the work of the single most important post-war German artist, Joseph Beuys. Beuys used actual dead hares in a number of performances or 'actions', most notoriously in *How to Explain Pictures to a Dead Hare* (1965), which according to his biographer, Heiner Stachelhaus, proceeded as follows:

Francis Bacon, *Triptych Inspired by the Oresteia of Aeschylus*, 1981, oil on canvas.

opposite: left-hand panel enlarged.

> Beuys sat on a chair in one corner of the gallery, next to the entrance. He had poured honey over his head, to which he had then affixed fifty dollars' worth of gold leaf. In his arms he cradled a dead hare, which he looked at

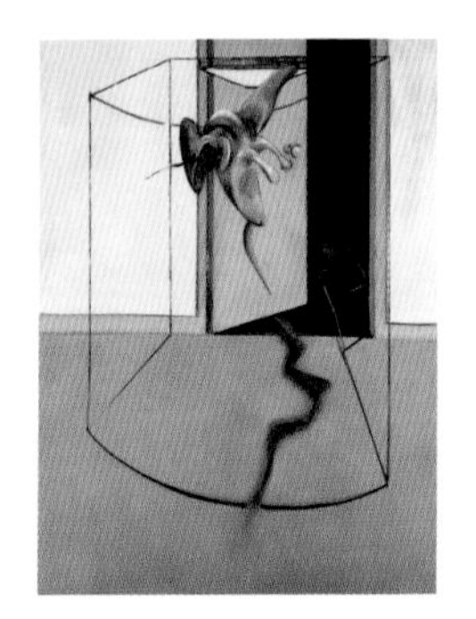

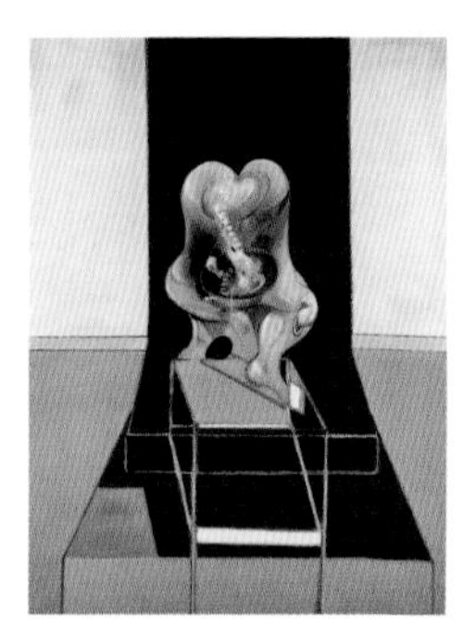

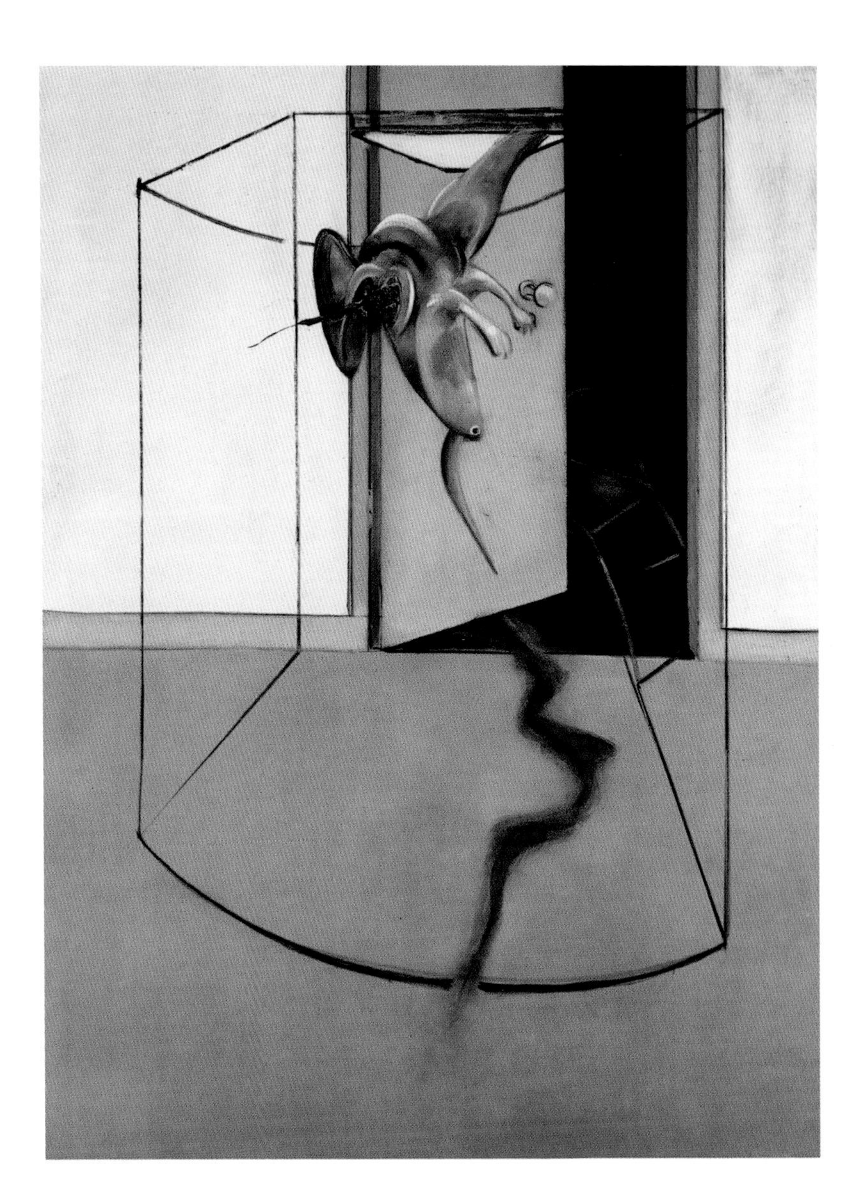

> steadfastly. Then he stood up, walked around the room holding the dead hare in his arms, and held it up close to the pictures on the walls; he seemed to be talking to it. Sometimes he broke off his tour and, still holding the dead creature, stepped over a withered fir tree that lay in the middle of the gallery. All this was done with indescribable tenderness and great concentration.[18]

In another piece, *EURASIA Siberian Symphony*, he moved a dead hare stilted on rods around a gallery space, and carried out a number of baffling manoeuvres involving a blackboard, thermometer, rubber tube and white powder. In *The Chief* he lay wrapped in felt for eight hours on a gallery floor, uttering non-semantic, animalistic sounds into a microphone, with a dead hare placed at his feet while another lay next to his head. These were only the most strangely spectacular of what might be called Beuys's hare works, a series that was augmented throughout his career, in a variety of media. In the early 1960s he had invented a colour, 'Braunkreuz', which consisted of housepaint mixed with hares' blood, and in 1971 he exhibited *Hare's Blood*, a small amount of the blood of a hare mounted in a triangular plastic slide. Beuys utilized hare body parts in his *Burned Door, Beak and Ears of a Hare* (1953) and *Cross with Kneecap and Hare's Skull* (1961). In the early 1980s he used a tin chocolate mould in the shape of a hare to make *Hare with Sun*, in which fake jewels from a dismantled replica crown of Ivan the Terrible were set into a wall space to give the impression of a nest lined by the hare with the crown parts. His plasticine hare and toy soldier on the Green Party poster designed in the late 1970s was adapted from an earlier work, *The Invincible* (1963). In *Hare Stone* he painted a gold rudimentary outline of a running hare on a basalt block. A hare figures in his *A Political Party for Animals*,

Joseph Beuys in a performance of *How to Explain Pictures to a Dead Hare*, 1965.

and as the logo for the Free International University for Creativity and Interdisciplinary Research which he co-founded.

As in the many works employing 'Braunkreuz', so the 'idea' of the hare was utilized or evoked in other pieces in which no actual image of the animal is evident. *Hare's Grave* is made up of various bits junk and fat stuck to a board; *Back Support for a Fine-limbed Person (Hare Type) of the 20th Century AD* is an iron cast based upon a device made for a disabled child. Two of Beuys's signature sculptural materials were fat and felt, the latter used with an awareness that much felt was made from hare fur. With this in mind a large number of other works can be appended to the above list, including his felt suit and door wedge, as well as works in which he wrapped, respectively, a piano, a TV, a radio and a samurai sword in felt. The hare is not the only animal to appear serially in Beuys's work. He also produced works in which the bee and stag assume a totemic status within his vast and varied oeuvre. But it is the one to which he seemingly attached most importance, even to the point of conceiving of it as a kind of alter ego. In one of those 1960s statements which is poised like his 'actions' between provocative absurdity and seriousness, between would-be shamanic profundity and jest, he went so far as to assert that 'I am not a human being, I am a hare'.[19]

Why the hare, for Beuys? When *The Chief* was performed for the second time the noises uttered by him were broadcast onto the still ruined streets of Berlin. His radically 'expanded concept' of sculpture is underwritten and supported by an equally radical politics, and both emerge from the aftermath of the Second World War perceived as a kind of degree zero demanding not just new forms of art but of perception and consciousness. Sooner or later when looking at his work it's necessary to consider the way in which it arises from the actual and ideological rubble of post-war Germany, and in seeking to account for his choice of the hare as a recurrent motif, prop and provider of *materia* there is no better starting point than his own account of his wartime experience. According to Beuys he was born or 'reborn' as an artist when his fighter plane crashed in the Crimea and he was rescued by Tartar tribesmen who wrapped his burned body in animal fat and felt. The strict veracity of this account has been questioned. What is certain is that he volunteered for the Luftwaffe, saw action, was injured and was awarded the Iron Cross. Whether true in its details or not, his account of the crash constitutes a remarkable piece of myth-making in which he is translated in a near-death experience from Nazi uniform to the healing integument provided by a 'primitive' and shamanistic Eurasian culture. In addition there was the 'irreversible shock' Beuys subsequently experienced on learning of the Nazi death camps, which he described as his 'basic experience since the end of the War'.[20] No doubt one of the things he learned of was that, after 1942, human hair was being taken from Holocaust victims and shipped to German-owned factories to make felt.

Beuys was keen to point out that as an artist he worked with materials rather than with symbols, and to develop the notion that felt, fat, dead animals, copper, sulphur, honey, blood, bones could provide 'matter for thought'. His own thinking about felt gave it special significance as an insulator and a kind of battery storing 'spiritual warmth or the beginning of an evolution'. Similarly with 'Braunkreuz', he did not consider it a colour so much as a generic medium for sculptural expression, evoking the earth as a protective medium (as well as blood, rust and excrement). His most explicit statement about the animal which provided blood for 'brown cross' and fur for felt is a characteristic mixture of natural history, myth and obscure logic:

Joseph Beuys, *EURASIA, Siberian Symphony*, 1963. Panel with chalk drawing, felt and fat, hare and blue painted poles.

The hare has things in common with the stag but has a very different specialization in matters of the blood. While the stag's province is from the middle of the body up to the head, the hare relates more to the lower part of the body, so in particular he has a strong affinity to women, to birth and to menstruation, and generally to chemical transformation of blood. That's what the hare demonstrates to us all when he hollows out his form: the movement of incarnation. The hare incarnates himself into the earth, which is what we human beings can only radically achieve with our thinking: he rubs, pushes, digs himself into Materia (earth); finally he penetrates its laws, and

> through his work his thinking is sharpened then transformed, and becomes revolutionary.[21]

Though hardly essential for viewing Beuys's hare works, this is a passage which has value for what it reveals about the kind of thinking which informed them. It contains elements that are politically vulnerable (the unwittingly reactionary move from 'lower part of the body' to 'a strong affinity with women') and others that will hardly do as natural history, if looked at literal-mindedly (the exaggeration, or worse, of the extent to which hares 'dig into' the earth; the unexplained reference to 'chemical transformation of blood'). Yet it shows how Beuys's thinking about hares constituted an attempt to let back in and elaborate perceptions prevalent in pre-Linnaean and pre-Enlightenment natural history, in combination with a modern fascination with their creaturely 'otherness' and a commitment to explore and learn from non-human modes of being and perception. The key elements in Beuys's thinking about the hare in particular, as revealed in his statement, are its *closeness to the earth*, femininity (recalling Jung on the hare as a 'feminine principle') and mysteriousness.

In one of the earliest hare works, a hare's ears are hung from a charred wooden door like some kind of apotropaic charm from a rural outhouse. They also suggest the living animal's supersensitivity, and the beginning therefore of the theme in Beuys's work of the necessity for a post-war 'listening in' to or heightened awareness of the natural world, with the burned door relating to the war itself rather than to the aftermath of a non-specific fire. Similarly, in *How to Explain Pictures . . .* Beuys placed beneath his chair a 'radio' consisting of a wired- up animal bone. Two of the hare actions attempt most fully to dramatize this coming into contact with animal forms of existence, *How to*

Explain Pictures . . . apparently staging an absurd failure or impossibility of communication, and *The Chief* effecting a shamanistic switching off of our own range of semantics in order to commune with an obscurely known or unknowable one.

Stachelhaus has interpreted *How to Explain Pictures . . .* as providing an image of the artist silently mouthing to a mute animal

Joseph Beuys, German Green Party poster adapted by the artist from his work, *The Invincible*, 1979.

what cannot be said to fellow men. It is more interesting, however, to note the ways in which its pathos works in directions other than towards this slightly kitsch or cliched conception of the 'misunderstood' artist, or artist without means of communication. On one level the 'indescribable tenderness' with which Beuys handles the hare embodies the kind of relationship towards the natural world which was to lead to Beuys's espousal of green politics, with the withered tree at the centre of the piece 'standing for' the animal's intimate connection to the environment. On another the piece partakes of that secret narrative in Beuys's work which has to do with obliquely evoking and mourning Nazi atrocities. He may or may not have known that children born in the Warsaw ghetto were referred to as 'hares', or of the tradition of depicting the persecution of Jews with images of hunted hares, or again, of the image of hounds in Paul Celan's 'Death Fugue'.[22] Even the grim connection between felt and the Holocaust, of which he was acutely aware, is not necessarily alluded to in the piece. And yet the act of mourning for the dead animal, with head anointed (albeit with honey and gold leaf rather than ashes) is susceptible to interpretation with regard to the still-raw subject of the war's human dead, with the hare used in its traditional role as quintessential victim. Similarly, in *The Chief* Beuys might be seen to have donned the felt blanket like a hair shirt in some equally obscure expiation. The action clearly refers to his own autobiographical myth of being reborn as an artist at the same time as he was invalided out of the war, and both *The Chief* and *How to Explain Pictures...* contain elements of staging national rebirth in the aftermath of war, emergency and rampant militarism: by appealing to tenderness, radically 'other' modes of perception and to a searching inwardness.

Some of the simpler hare works provide evidence of related themes. In *DDR Hase* (or *German Democratic Republic Hare*) Beuys

used an image of an overweight captive animal to satirically symbolize post-war Germany. By wrapping felt around an iron rod in *Samurai Sword* he enacted the insulation or neutralization of the negative energy of the metal, with the title of the piece alluding to the militaristic uses of iron. *The Invincible* wittily combines a number of elements, with its naively fashioned 'home-made' plasticine hare confronting mass-produced metal toy soldier on a dust-strewn white ground. In combination with the title the contrast in scale between the two figures – the hare magnified to relatively huge proportions – suggests a subversion of the animal's status as quintessential victim, or a magnification in accordance with the 'victim's' moral and spiritual superiority to the tiny militaristic figure. In *Hare With Sun*, too, it is surely no accident that it is the crown of Ivan the Terrible (the same tyrant that Eisenstein used in his coded anti-Nazi film) that is dismantled to line the hare's nest, in an image of a tricksterish 'victory' over tyrannical power.

In other works it is the fragility of the animal that is uppermost. *Hare's Grave* is at one obvious level a hyperbolic image of a throwaway consumer society piling its junk upon the 'natural' environment; *Young Hare* a depiction of a leveret that is so delicately faint that it seems on the verge of disappearance, or conveys something of the tenuous nature of the creature's coming into being. Elsewhere Beuys combines allusions to the physical characteristics of the hare with variously resonant contrasting materials. *Harestone* works by superimposing the agility and speed of a hare in flight upon a massive piece of solid basalt. *Back Support for a Fine-Limbed Person* . . . is altogether more mysterious and poetic, inviting as it does a comparison between human and lagomorph form and physicality. The title gives the piece an almost archaeological or anthropological aspect, as if the object were an exhibit in some distant post-twentieth-century gathering

Joseph Beuys, *Back Support for a Fine-Limbed Person (Hare Type) of the 20th Century AD*, 1970–72, cast iron.

Joseph Beuys, *Cross with Kneecap and Hare's Skull*, 1961, bronze and bone.

of its artefacts. A certain pathos is added when we learn that the 'back-rest' is a cast taken from a device used to support a disabled child, with the consequent contrast this sets up between the athleticism of the hare and the condition of the child for whom it was designed, though the main idea in play seems to be a more general though equally pointed false rhyme between the free and superlative physicality of the hare and the human frame, however 'fine-limbed'.

When Beuys hung an actual hare's skull on a bronze cross it's likely that he did so partly in allusion to the Christian iconography of the hare, though his piece has the appearance of some primitive counter-icon or result of a fusion between Christian and pagan traditions. It is as if, for Beuys, the hare has sufficient *numen* or mysterious resonance from the range of its traditional associations to compete with or supplement the cross, rather than functioning here as an element of simple profanation. Beuys drew upon the symbolic power of the cross by using a modified form of it in numerous works, sometimes painted in Braunkreuz where the hare is materially present in the form of blood, or cut from felt where it is similarly present in the form of matted fur. In his performance piece *Directional Forces* he also worked with the animal's traditional (Buddhist) lunar associations, by way of a light box illuminating a photograph of the 'hare in the moon'.

When the art critic Robert Hughes interpreted Robert Rauschenberg's stuffed goat wearing a car tyre as an allegory of homosexuality, Rauschenberg commented contemptuously that 'a stuffed goat is special in the way that a stuffed goat is special' – a way of dismissing all such searches for hidden meaning in the work.[23] Beuys, on the other hand, despite his disclaimer to work with 'materials' rather than symbols (a standard modernist

Barry Flanagan, *Large Leaping Hare, 1982*, bronze and steel.

manoeuvre) can be seen to have brought into play with regard to the hare works many of the animal's symbolic, metaphoric and other resonances, pushing them into politically charged new territory.

Compared to the disturbing if lushly agonized hares of Soutine and the complex variety of Beuys's uses of the hare, the Welsh artist Barry Flanagan's monumental hare sculptures are notable for their celebratory, gravity-defying lightness. Flanagan was first drawn to the hare as a subject after reading *The Leaping Hare*, and seems to have responded in particular to that work's account of the animal's symbolic and mythic associations with vitality, combined with a sculptural fascination with its lithe form and motor system, and further, via an interest in Alfred Jarry's absurdist anti-philosophy, 'pataphysics', with the animal's 'anarchic' tendencies. The graceful forms of his leaping or running hares are typically and dynamically contrasted in his work with an architectural, geometrical, or heavily solid man-made form: a pyramid, the Empire State Building, large bells, anvils, a military helmet, cones and crescents. One of the best and earliest of what was to become a popular, signature series – *Hare and Pyramid* – possibly alludes to the Egyptian hieroglyph for 'to-be', with its gravity-defying, elongated hare leaping over a stylized, gilded pyramidal form. The same cast of a hare was used twenty years later for *Six-foot Leaping Hare on Empire State*, possibly in response to the 9/11 attack on New York.

In *Hare and Helmet*, by placing an unnaturally standing, anthropomorphized hare upon military headgear, Flanagan also evokes in simplified form one of the themes explored by Beuys. We might even detect in *Hare and Bell* (with its huge church-tower-type bronze-cast bell being leaped over) an allusion to the hare's place in Christian symbolism. Various drum-playing hares recall a medieval illustration of the animal with a tabor,

Francisco Toledo, *Crafty Hare*, 1988, mixed media on *amate* (bark) paper.

and the tradition, carried even into the nineteenth century, of such trained 'musical' hares appearing in sideshows. In his various *Nijinski* hares, such as *Left and Right-handed Nijinski on Anvil Point*, there seems to be a pun at work linking the madness of the dancer and the hare's reputation for both melancholy and exuberant, harebrained and 'mad March' behaviour. A number of anthropomorphized hare-acrobats play variations upon the theme of graceful athleticism and balance present in almost all of Flanagan's hare works, though by no means all of them succeed in avoiding a fall into anthropomorphic kitsch. As is the case with his series of cricket-playing hares.

Other artists such as Sophie Ryder have made serial sculptures of hares, or in her case 'hare-women', morphed figures which have lithe human bodies and the heads of hares. In certain of these works such figures are placed in relation to hounds or to hybrid masculine forms, including minotaurs, putting into play themes of human/animal hybridity and gender stereotype. A recent piece by an Irish sculptor – bronze hares boxing with outsize erect penises – seems designed to give back a scandalous edge to the animal lacking in those leaping, boxing, or moon-gazing sculpted or cast hares which are to be found in galleries selling art to the public all over Britain. In the work of the Mexican painter and sculptor, Francisco Toledo, conspicuously sexualized as well as trickster-like hares can be found copulating with, fellating and buggering human figures, in a literalization of their

Francisco Toledo, *Hare*, 1980, acrylic on ostrich egg.

opposite: Sam Taylor-Wood, *Self-portrait in a Single Breasted Suit with Hare*, 2001, c-type print.

symbolic associations with sex. One of his paintings is of a lagomorph possessing four erect penises, two as ears; one of his sculptures has a hare astride a cannon in the shape of a penis. His use of the hare also extends to his more strangely resonant *Hare and Death,* in which a human skeleton excretes a spiral in which a hare is sitting.

In one of the most striking recent art works which activates or alludes to some of the animal's symbolic power, Sam Taylor-Wood has photographed herself holding upright by its back legs a large stuffed hare. The image thus inverts the position of the animal as portrayed in the tradition of still-life and game painting, and by doing so turns on its head, so to speak, the *memento mori* aspect which it has there, converting it instead into a life-against-death trope. This is reinforced by the work's title, *Self-portrait in Single Breasted Suit with Hare,* with its wittily defiant allusion to the fact that it was made after she survived cancer. She has referred in an interview to her awareness of the fact that the animal is also a 'symbol of lust' in many paintings, and that 'In my mind this very erect, stiff hare masculinised me'.[24] So that as well as inverting the usual association with death, in order to make an image of narrow escape and survival, she has also inverted the set of associations the hare has with femininity, in order to reinforce the work as one to do with defiant *agency* rather than victimhood. Her video *A Little Death,* with its hare left to decay in front of a fixed camera, graphically realizes one of the themes of still-life painting containing hares. Of this second work, made just before the *Self-portrait,* she has commented that her own first viewing of it was an experience of 'rough decay', of 'pure violence', of 'the most disturbing film I'd ever seen.'[25] The *Self-portrait,* by contrast, seems to be all about control, with the rough violence and pure decay arrested. And contrary to the would-be shamanistic communing with animals in Beuys, or the celebratory acceptance of that 'animality' shared by humans, via sex, in Toledo, it's an image which holds animality at arm's length, with its sitter in dandyishly chic black suit, standing on a marble floor and with her other hand on the button of a remote link to the camera, and an additional visual pun – her running shoes – has the artist 'up and running' after cancer, in a triumph of art over nature, albeit one which resonates in a sophisticated way with the shared animal mortality of hare and sitter. And one which, deliberately or not, is reinforced by the further appropriateness of the chosen animal which derives from its associations with resurrection, with proto-medicine (including cures for cancer) and with creativity.

5 Hare Poetry, Hare Thought

There is apparently an old Welsh saying or proverb which states that 'a hare is hare': a nice antidote to the co-opting of the animal into all kinds of slippery symbolic and other signification, perhaps, though one which also begs the question as to what that animal simply 'is'. It has been calculated that of all proverbs involving animals, roughly seven per cent involve hares. You can't hold with the hare and run with the hounds (a saying most suggestively run with by Father Ronald Knox: 'the humanist runs with the hare, the satirist hunts with the hounds'); to hunt or chase two hares at once means to pursue two activities neither of which is likely to succeed. To 'start a few hares' means to set in train thoughts or activities in a preliminary or sketchy fashion, or in a manner in which they are not followed to their logical, satisfactory or foreseen conclusion. There is a medieval Latin phrase, '*hic jacet lepus*', literally 'here the hare leaps', used to signify 'here's the crux of the problem' by analogy to the animal's elusiveness and unpredictability. To be 'hare-brained' is a matter of 'having or showing no more "brains" or sense than a hare', to be 'heedless, reckless; rash, wild, mad'. Its current usage, most common in the clichéd phrase 'hare-brained scheme' is a pale reflection of the uses to which it has been historically put. 'Harebrainnesse' for one late sixteenth-century writer 'hath ridiculous, furious and phantasticall motions', where 'phantasticall' connotes

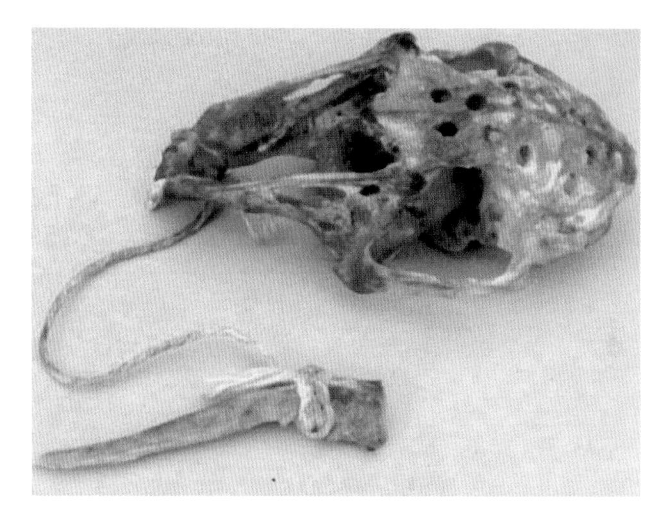

Labrador Inuit toy, *c.* 1921. A player must flip the Arctic hare skull and impale it with the hare's leg bone as it falls, through one of the holes drilled in the top of the skull.

a dangerous because misleading aspect of the imagination.[1] In Christopher Marlowe's 'Hero and Leander' it could be used with even greater severity: 'In gentle breasts/ Relenting thoughts and pity rests./ And who have hard hearts, and obdurate minds,/ But vicious, hare-brained, and illiterate hinds.'[2]

On the other hand it could be embraced and turned into a positive attribute. Shakespeare's Portia in *The Merchant of Venice* runs metaphorically with such a possibility: 'The brain may devise laws for the blood, but a hot temper leaps o'er a cold decree: such a hare is madness, the youth, to skip o'er the meshes of good counsel the cripple', though only before adding that 'this reasoning is not in the fashion to choose me a husband.'[3] When Laurence Sterne has the narrator of *Tristram Shandy* chastise himself for 'rash jerks, and hare-brain'd squirts',[4] we are predisposed to see the phrase as an endearingly positive description of the novel's peculiar style and construction rather than as a *mea culpa* to be taken at face value. A close reader of

Typus Logica, from *Margarita Philosophica* by Gregorious Reisch, 1503.

Sterne, James Joyce, the author of *Finnegans Wake*, one of the least straightforward works in or out of the English language, has occasion at one point to devise the phrase 'the hare and turtle pen and paper', giving to his own 'pen' and the relentlessly punning or doubling nature of his text a hare-like quality. This is echoed elsewhere in the book by the phrase 'ear canny hare for doubling', which plays upon the 'doubling' of the hare's tracks in concealment or escape, and the auditory and conceptual doubling which is essential to all puns.[5]

The association of the hare with madness – first with 'melancholy', and then, probably via its proverbially 'mad March' or testosterone-driven mating behaviour, with more manic forms – is continuous with its use of an emblem for 'illogicality'. John Layard's account of it as a figure for intuition, a faculty involving 'leaps to conclusions (whether right or wrong)',[6] represents an ingenious positive recovery of its valence as an emblem of non-logical human thought processes. Though he does not mention the fact in his book there is, intriguingly, an emblematic tradition of depicting logical thinking itself as a hare hunt. In one of the most elaborate of these emblems 'Dame Logica', a huntress on horseback, is shown chasing the hare *Problema* with her greyhounds *Veritas* and *Falsitas*. In order that there should be no doubt as to what is depicted the meaning of everything in the image is spelt out, so that the problematic hare runs with the actual word *Problema* written on its side. The landscape in which the hunt takes place includes the 'forest of opinions', and the covert of *Insolubilia*, while rocks are labelled 'linguistic fallacies' and 'extra linguistic fallacies', while the huntress blows the horn 'spoken word' from which two 'premisses' in the form of roses emerge. The hare-hunt is chosen as the vehicle for this didactic memory picture (rather than the deer-hunt or pursuit of other game) because of a convergence of factors which include the animal's reputation for scatty, mad or illogical behaviour as well as elusiveness and speed. Its actually 'problematic' as well as allegorical status within it is backed up by a tradition of ascribing to canine intelligence a logical capacity which is frequently illustrated with reference to hunting dogs' ability to track hares. Aelian was one of the first to make such an argument, in a fashion elaborated in the following terms by Topsell:

> Dogges have reason, & use logick in their hunting, for they will cast about for game, as a disputant doth for truth, as if they should say either the Hare is gone on the left hand, or on the right hand, or straight forward. Whereupon he runneth foorth right after the true and infallible footsteps of the Hare.[7]

Such extended metaphors or allegories as are in operation in the hare-hunting emblem may strike us as either leaden or ingenious, but the comparison between hunting and the operation of the human mind was so much in the mainstream that examples of it can be found in such eminent and influential discourses as Hobbes on the imagination or 'train of thoughts' and Dryden on imagination and wit, as well as in the work of the Spanish author Juan Huarte, an Elizabethan translation of which has been credited with introducing the idea of the 'swiftness' of the imaginative faculty into English.[8] When William Wordsworth reaches for a hare symbol at a key point in the lyric poem 'Resolution and Independence' he does so in order to transfer the agency and emphasis given to the dog in such metaphors onto the hare as a figure for the poet, in accordance with a sensibility and theory of imagination quite different from that held by Hobbes or by Dryden. Three twentieth-century examples of thinking with a hare-hound or hunted hare figure run with it in contrasting directions. For John Berger, the human imagination has 'difficulty remaining within the confines of a materialist philosophy', for it 'dreams, like a dog in its basket, of hares in the open'.[9] In his aphorism 'On the Law', Franz Kafka writes that 'The hunting dogs are playing in the courtyard, but the hare will not escape them, no matter how fast it may be flying already through the woods', a reflection upon the human condition as much as upon the sinister relentlessness of actual man-made

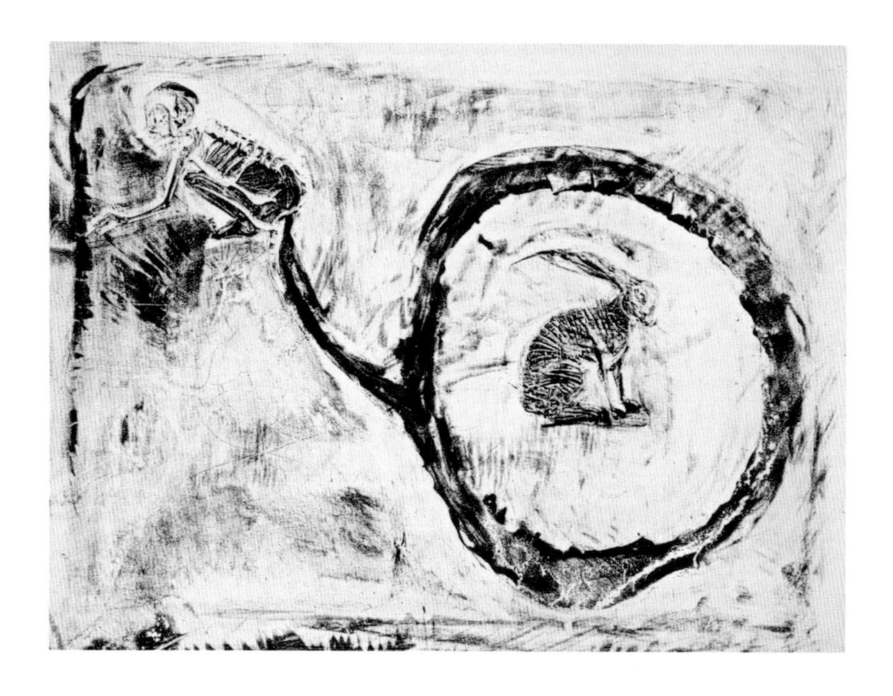

Francisco Toledo (b. 1940), *Hare and Death*, lithograph.

laws and of a 'law' of natural existence.[10] For the Chinese poet, Gu Cheng, the poet is 'like a hunter waiting beside a tree for hares to knock themselves out against it. After a while, he realizes that he is the hare.'[11]

The hare provides a figure for poetry, or for poetic thought, I would argue, both by analogy to its behaviour and in extension of its uses in emblems for logic and imagination. It is an apt figure for speed of thought and for associative thinking; for excluded middle terms and of connective discursive tissue (leaps from one thing to another) as well as for the somewhat mysterious and unpredictable elements required for its genuine composition. A line can be traced in poetry in English showing the development of intimations of its suitability for such use, which is parallel to the more overt development of sympathy for the actual animal and to the sophistication of its traditional symbolic valences via its increasingly naturalistic representation. The thirteenth-century manuscript poem, 'The Names of the Hare' throws a remarkable flurry of epithets at its quarry. Some are relatively naturalistic, or intended to be so, and would not be out of place in the work of those early natural historians who included 'appropriate' epithets in their accounts of animals ('swift as wind'; 'long-eared'; 'leaper'; 'purblind'; 'dew-sipper'); others more playful and folkish ('furze-cat'; 'stubble-stag'; 'shagger'; 'seeker of refuge with the lambs') and a third kind deriving from perceptions of the animal as sinister or out of left-field ('traitor'; 'covenant-breaker'; 'friendless one'; 'one who makes you shudder'). There is a nicely appropriate way in which the animal thus named eventually becomes nameless or unnameable, slipping away from this pile-up of names even as the poet voices his desire to meet it next 'in onion broth or bread':

> He who has 'Scoundrel' for a name
> The stag with the leathery horns
> The creature that dwells in the corn
> The creature that all men scorn
> The creature that none dare name.[12]

It is a poem which seems to delight in its subject's power and peculiarity and to fend off that power with buoyant humour and linguistic relish, even as it partakes in a genuine wariness regarding the hare's ominous character. The hares mentioned in William Langland's late fourteenth-century *Piers Plowman*, in contrast, crop up for their implication in socio-religious and legal discourse: satirically inasmuch as his Parson Sloth confesses to a preference for hunting hares over construing psalms, though without much humour in the suggestion that prelates who hunted them on a Sunday deserved capital punishment.[13] In the *General Prologue* to Chaucer's *Canterbury Tales* an ascription to his Monk of a fondness for hare-hunting convicts him of both suspect worldliness and something worse besides, via the traditional punning on the double meaning of 'venery':

> Grehoundes he had as swift as fowel in flight;
> Of prikyng and of hunting for the hare
> Was all his lust, for no cost wold he spare.[14]

There is a fifteenth-century English poem which provides an early instance of sympathy for the hunted hare and of the notion of it as a kind of universal or quintessential victim:

> There is no beast in the world, I ween,
> Hart, hind, buck, ne doe,
> That suffers half so much teen
> As doth the silly Wat, go where he go![15]

The hare's 'silliness' is emphasized here as part of a developing tendency to emphasize in verse its innocuous character, and to downplay or simply exclude both its powers of defence and, *pace* 'The Names of the Hare', its negatively folkloric associations. For the author of 'The Hare, to the Hunter', it is 'A sillie beast that cannot make defence', as well as one which is scarcely worth the taking for utilitarian purposes, much less so from a moral point of view:

> For first my skinne is scarcely worth a placke,
> My fleshe is drie, and hard for to endew,
> My greace (God knoweth) not great upon my backe,

> My selfe, and all, that is within me founde,
> Is neyther, good, great, ritche, fatte, sweete, nor sounde.[16]

Shakespeare's *Venus and Adonis*, on the other hand, initiates the kind of relatively naturalistic description and detail which was to become typical in later seventeenth-century and eighteenth-century verse (albeit taken from the hunting manuals rather than from first-hand observation); accords respect to the hare for its independent power and compares the animal near exhaustion, with empathy rather than anthropomorphism, to 'one sore sick that hears the passing-bell'. And further, though it would be anachronistic to see the hare 'indenting with the way' as containing an allusion to a page of text ('indenting' did not become a printer's term until the mid nineteenth century) there is an ascription to the hare of 'wit' which links it to writing:

> He cranks and crosses with a thousand doubles:
> The many musits through which he goes
> Are like a labyrinth to amaze his foes.
> Sometimes he runs among a flock of sheep,
> To make the cunning hounds mistake their smell,
> And sometimes sorteth with a herd of deer;
> Danger deviseth shifts; wit waits on fear . . .[17]

The hare's 'maziness' is highlighted to such an extent by later writers as to suggest a naturalistic detail hovering on the verge of a figure for poetry itself. For poetry that proceeds, to adapt John Donne's phrase, by indirection to find direction out. Somervile's hunted hare constructs 'maze within maze' which the hounds must 'unravel'; Thomson's an 'early labyrinth' in 'scented dew'; John Gay's 'doubles to mis-lead the hound,/ And measures back her mazy round'. A late twentieth-century poem by Paul Muldoon can be seen to complete the idea, with its meta-poetic contrast between 'the shortest distance between two points' – a straight line – and a hare 'That goes by leaps and bounds/ Across the grazing,/ Here and there, / This way and that, by single-minded swervings'.[18]

William Cowper famously took poetic sympathy for the hare as far as to keep several in his house, writing a prose account of his experience with them which was still much read and admired in the nineteenth century and a poem, 'Epitaph on a Hare', which is the most anthologized of his works. In his long poem 'The Task', he has recourse to his hare experience in specifically anti-hunting terms ('Detested sport . . . One shelter'd hare/ Has never heard the sanguinary yell/ Of cruel man . . .')[19]; in the epitaph the focus is more celebratory and designed to emphasize the limited extent to which one particular hare has been domesticated and tamed. For Cowper it is important that the animal has retained its essential wildness, even as he constructs a chamber version of an Adamic idyll of congress between man and beast:

> Though duly from my hand he took
> His pittance every night,
> He did it with a jealous look,
> And, when he could, would bite.[20]

The poem wittily avoids the kind of cloying sentimentality endemic to the genre of elegies on the death of pets, and is deepened by a subtle, sub-textual identification between 'wild jack hare' 'to domestic bounds confined', and the poet's struggle with mental illness. Though understated in the poem itself ('he would oft beguile/ My heart of thoughts that made it ache'), it is surely no accident that he began to keep his hares soon after a period of confinement in a mental institution. Taming, to a degree, an animal proverbially 'hare-brained' and subject to its own periods of 'Mad March' behaviour was a peculiarly apt form of both actual and symbolic 'therapy'. Edward Lear seems to have Cowper in mind, and to have made something like this interpretation, in his own comic-melancholic style, in a limerick illustrated with a pained figure riding an outsized hare:

> There was an old man whose despair
> Induced him to purchase a hare
> Whereon one fine day,
> He rode wholly away,
> Which partly assuaged his despair.[21]

Lear's verse, like Lewis Carroll's, contains elements which parody 'Romantic' poetry. In what has become one of the set pieces of English Romanticism, Wordsworth reaches for a hare symbol in order to make his own identification between it and workings of the (poetic) mind. 'Resolution and Independence' begins by creating a kind of idyll subsequent to a night-storm:

Edward Lear's old man in despair riding wholly away on a hare, from *More Nonsense Pictures, Rhymes and Botany &c.*, 1872.

Lewis Carroll's *Mad Hatter and March Hare,* cramming the dormouse into a teapot, in Tenniel's illustration to *Alice's Adventures in Wonderland.*

> All things that love the sun are out of doors;
> The sky rejoices in the morning's birth;
> The grass is bright with rain-drops; on the moors
> The Hare is running races in her mirth;
> And with her feet she from the plashy earth
> Raises a mist; which, glittering in the sun,
> Runs with her all the way, wherever she doth run.[22]

With the peculiar detail of the sun illuminating the mist raised by the running hare, Wordsworth seems to be remembering the biblical post-Flood rainbow that signalled the new covenant between man and God. That we are in symbolic as well as naturalistic territory is indicated by making the actually nocturnal and crepuscular creature one of those that 'love the sun'. Be that as it may, the poem goes on to make a direct link between the hare that 'rac'd with joy', the poetic and childhood possession of 'joy' (a key Wordsworthian term), and the descent into a kind of post-lapsarian dejection:

> But, as it sometimes chanceth, from the might
> Of joy in minds that cannot farther go,
> As far as we have mounted in delight
> In our dejection do we sink as low,
> To me that morning did it happen so;
> And fears, and fancies, thick upon me came;
> Dim sadness, and blind thoughts I knew not nor could name.
>
> I heard the Sky-lark singing in the sky;
> And I bethought me of the playful Hare;
> Even such a happy Child of earth am I;
> Even as these blissful Creatures do I fare;
> Far from the world I walk, and from all care;
> But there may come another day to me,
> Solitude, pain of heart, distress, and poverty.

If the hare with its vitality and unselfconscious participation in a kind of world spirit provides an apt figure for 'bliss', the fact that its life is actually determined by its status as a prey species is apt too, along with its reputation for 'melancholy' and 'sleeplesseness', for the subsequent conversion of 'happy Child of earth' (poet and hare) into doomed figure, via the death of the poet Thomas Chatterton:

> I thought of Chatterton, the marvellous Boy,
> The sleepless Soul that perish'd in its pride . . .
>
> We poets in our youth begin in gladness
> But thereof comes in the end despondency and madness.

In 'Hares at Play', a sonnet by John Clare, a poet, like Cowper, subject to periods of actual and instituitonalized 'madness', there is a contrast between hares that nocturnally 'sturt', 'like happy thoughts', before being startled by milk-maidens who

> Gingle their yokes and sturt them in the corn
> Through well-known beaten paths each nimbling hare
> Sturts quick as fear – and seeks its hidden lair.[23]

Clare's folkish idyll, with its repetition of a vernacular word for the technical hunting term for raising a hare, 'start', though more realistic and less highly strung than Wordsworth's, retains both an identification with the animal and a use of its symbolic valence as first essence of animal well-being and then essence of fear. Fleeting appearances of hares in his work are also informed by an alertness to their social significance as preserved or protected quarry. In a letter of 1824 he describes a 'pleasant walk' curtailed by the onset of the shooting season, with 'poor hares and pheasants and partridges flying in all directions', adding that 'panic struck they put me in mind of the inhabitants of a Village flying before an invading enemy'. In this conversion of massacred hares and birds into human inhabitants of the countryside –more specifically, we can assume, its rural labourers and poor – Clare includes himself by writing that 'I was forced to return home fearing I might be shot under the hedges'.[24]

What we have in certain of these poetic hares is an interiorization of the animal's more straightforward emblematic and symbolic valences, a process no more beautifully achieved than with Emily Dickinson's use of a hound-hare figure in 'This Heart that Broke so Long', a poem which combines epitaph or hymn-like simplicity with searching inwardness; steadfastness in faith, or love, with no answering reality:

Sophie Ryder, *Introspective*, 2004, life-size wire figures.

This heart that broke so long –
These feet that never flagged –
This faith that watched for star in vain,
Give gently to the dead –

Hound cannot overtake the Hare
That fluttered, panting, here –
Nor any schoolboy rob the nest
Tenderness builded there.[25]

Or more wittily run with than in Apollinaire's epigram on the hare from his *Bestiary,* which urges its reader to be 'not cowardly and lewd/ Like the buck hare and lover' but to have a brain, or mind, 'like the doe hare/ Which conceives again while pregnant'.[26] The fragile hare which appears in the first of Rimbaud's *Illuminations,* uttering 'a prayer to the rainbow through the spider's web', is a totem animal for the work's visionary flight.[27] There has been in contemporary British and Irish poetry something of a minor population explosion in hares, in inverse proportion to the population decline in actual hares, partly enabled by the putting back into general currency the material collected in *The Lady of The Hare* and *The Leaping Hare,* but also, I suspect, down to perceptions of it as a peculiarly 'poetic' animal. There is Seamus Heaney's version of 'The Names of the Hare'; David Harsent's sequence 'Lepus', his libretto for Harrison Birtwhistle's *The Woman and The Hare,* and a further sequence with the same title; Dorothy Molloy's *Hare Soup*; the hare in the title poem of Ian Duhig's *The Lammas Hireling* (a volume which uses Dürer's 'Young Hare' on the cover) and in the title poem of Bernard O'Donoghue's *Outliving* (a volume which uses a medieval image of hares hunting sportsmen on its cover); Paul Muldoon's hares, and the fact that other collections have used as cover-images Sidney Nolan's *Hare in Trap* and the running hare from Pisanello's *Vision of St Eustace* – as well as the first publication of T. S. Eliot's *Inventions of the March Hare,* and so on.[28] There is also Ted Hughes's poem 'The Hare', itself an addition to the hares in his short stories 'The Harvesting' (in which a huntsman mysteriously becomes the hare which he shoots) and 'Difficulties of a Bridegroom', and to fleeting appearances of the animal in his work such as the one in which it is described as proceeding 'like a root, going deeper'.[29]

Hughes's animal poems have been conventionally read as part of the poet's attempt to uncover a kind of 'deep' England – linguistic, imaginative, historical, not without political design and resonance – in reaction to the perceived narrowness, politeness, witty academicism and generally lowered horizons to which English verse had supposedly succumbed in the 1950s. 'The Hare' is continuous with that project in its relentless unearthing of the animal's folkloric valences, and is shot through with remembered reading and echoes of Lawrence's *Birds, Beasts and Flowers* (1923), of *The Leaping Hare*, and in its use of a flurry of epithets, of 'The Names of the Hare'. For Hughes the hare is 'That weird long-eared elf'; 'druid soul'; 'fairy woman'; 'dream beast'; 'kangaroo of the March corn'; 'witch maiden'. And then, in Lawrentian tones, but with echoes too of Blake and Christopher Smart, and a side-glance at Dürer:

Barry Flanagan, *Hare and Bell*, bronze, 1988.

The hare's bones are light as glass. And her face –

Who lifted her face to the Lord?
Her new-budded nostrils and lips,
For the daintiest pencillings, the last eyelash touches

Delicate as the down of a moth[30]

Or rather, this is Hughes's jill hare, for his fascination with and celebration of the animal's delicacy and power is made along gendered lines: the delicacy to the female, the power to the male:

With his Leaping-Legs, his Power-Thighs
Much too powerful for ordinary walking,
So powerful
They seem almost a burden, almost a problem.

A poem, then, which combines will-to-accuracy with regard to actual hares (the description of their unsuitedness to 'ordinary walking' is brilliantly and originally exact, as is the description of a hare careering on a road, in front of a following car, which 'can't keep his steering, in his ramshackle go-cart') with a sophisticated if sightly overcooked reprise of their reputation for 'uncanniness', as well as one which strikingly renews certain traditional observations. For it is one thing to compare the cry of a hare to that of a child, another to have a knocked-down lepus become, with its cries of human pain, 'a human baby on the road/ That you hardly dare pick up'. One thing, again, to cite the belief that hares predict changes in weather, another to write of one with 'Her black-tipped hairs *hearin*g tomorrow's weather' (my emphasis). In its attempt to resume and revivify hare lore, to cover the ground of its cultural representations even as it gives

A competitor in the Pursuit Race in Copenhagen, chasing a hare towards the finishing line, 1968.

vivid life to the animal itself, 'The Hare' doesn't fail to include an image of one pursued by a hound. Pursued but escaping, out of the written frame as much as away from the dog. It is an appropriate image with which to end the present study of an animal which has generated its variety of cultural constructions but remained elusive, indomitable, mysterious, mercurial, proceeding headlong and anarchically back into its proper sphere, by single-minded swervings.

Epilogue: Hare Writing

The hare, its eye all rods, sees everything
    in black and white. Runs all roads,
sits tight in its form, a narrow scrape,
    until the last minute. Is leaping from one thing
    to another, emblem of dialectic,
steering with its ears. Has *numen*, slaloms at night
on the A14 in your taxi's headlights.

Tell a captive hare it's to die in the morning,
    find it dead next day from the sheer
superfetating power of suggestion.
    Screams with the voice of a child when caught,
    is otherwise silent. Provided skin for parchment
in the age of illumination, and felt
to dampen piano hammers, in Victorian parlours.

'Electric Seal' to furriers – and Kropotkin
    with a natural anarchist, no friend
of the bourgeois rabbit. Called to witness
    at a witch-trial: houndstooth marks, forensic
    evidence, on the bruised thigh of a woman
hunted in the form of a hare. Is seeking
the gap or *smeuse* at the far end of the field

that will take it kicking into tomorrow,
Small bucket of blood pumping
through an outsize heart. Watch a hare in flight
for an idea of the limitations
of the human frame. Or a tracked hare weaving,
doubling its mazes of scent for the pack,
writing itself – now in, now out – of the picture.

Leaping hare from a 6th-century Byzantine floor mosaic, Israel.

Timeline of the Hare

25 MYA
Split of hares and rabbits from other lagomorphs

20,000 BC
Humans develop technology to trap Arctic hares

12,000 BC
Paleolithic cave painting of hare made at Le Gabillou, France

6,400–5,900 BC
Hittite vessel created in the shape of a hare

1502
Albrecht Dürer paints his *Young Hare* watercolour

1560s
Rules for hare coursing established by the Duke of Norfolk

1596
Hare described in medical treatise as single most useful animal in 'physicke'

1619
First monograph on hares, *Lagographia* by Wolfgang Waldung

1600–1740
Hares feature in still-life paintings by Snyders, Weenix, Chardin and others

1807
Wordsworth uses hare as cipher for natural 'joy' in his poem 'Resolution and Independence'

1836
First Waterloo Cup: it was to become the largest hare coursing event in Europe

1858
Darwin uses example of hounds adapting to hunt hares in first public outing of his theory of natural selection

1900–present
Number of brown hares declines significantly in Europe

1912
William Gidley publishes article providing basis for separation of lagomorphs from order *Rodentiae*

2,500 BC
Egyptian hieroglyph of hare meaning 'to be'

458 BC
Hare omen features in the *Oresteia* of Aeschylus

c. 450 BC
Biblical taboo placed on eating hare flesh

AD 60–61
Boudicca caries a live hare onto the battlefield for purposes of divination

c. 1400–1500
Hares figure as a pre-eminent quarry and 'most marvellous beast' in European hunting treatises

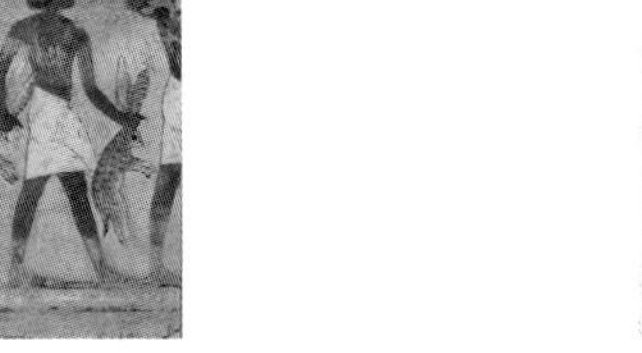

1653
Margaret Cavendish's 'The Hunting of the Hare' initiates a line of poetic protest against hare hunting

1733
Stephen Hales, in a pioneering work on blood circulation, uses hare as example of how 'timerous' animals have larger hearts than 'courageous' ones

1774
Horned hare included in Oliver Goldsmith's *History of Animated Nature*

1784
William Cowper writes 'Epitaph on a Hare', and an account of keeping three hares as pets

1944
Jungian psychologist John Layard publishes *The Lady of the Hare,* including influential essay on hares in world mythology

1953–84
Joseph Beuys creates a series of 'hare works', including *How to Explain Pictures to a Dead Hare*

2002
Sam Taylor-Wood exhibits her video *A Little Death*, a reworking of the hare motif in still-life painting

2004
Hare hunting banned in England and Wales, bringing law in line with most other European countries

References

1 *LAGOGRAPHIA CURIOSA*

1 Aelian, *On Animals*, trans. A. F. Scholfield (London, 1959), III, pp. 97–9.
2 Aristotle, *On the Generation of Animals*, trans. A. L. Peck (London, 1963), p. 453.
3 Aristotle, *Historia Animalium*, ed. J. A. Smith and W. D. Ross (Oxford, 1910), p. 579; p. 511.
4 Xenophon, *Cynegeticus*, ed. and trans. A. A. Phillips and M. M. Wilcock, in *Xenophon and Arrian On Hunting* (Warminster, 1999), p. 49.
5 Pliny the Elder, *Natural History*, English trans. H. Rackham et al. (London, 1938–63), VIII, pp. 151–4.
6 Albertus Magnus, *On Animals*, trans. Kenneth F. Kitchell Jr and Irven Michael Resnick (Baltimore and London, 1999), II, pp. 1515–16.
7 Edward Topsell, *The History of Four-footed Beasts* (London, 1658), pp. 207–17.
8 William Cogan, *The Haven of Health* (London, 1596), p. 120.
9 John Johnston, *A Description of the Nature of Four-footed Beasts*, trans. 'J. P.' (Amsterdam, 1678), p. 85.
10 Francis Bacon, *Of the Advancement of Learning* (New York, 1913), p. 29.
11 Francis Bacon, *Sylva Sylvarum, or, A Natural History in Ten Centuries* (London, 1627), p. 260.
12 Sir Thomas Browne, *Pseudodoxia Epidemica* (London, 1658), p. 120.

13 Georges-Louis Leclerc, Comte de Buffon, *Natural History, General and Particular*, trans. William Smellie (London, 1812), VI, p. 95.
14 Oliver Goldsmith, *A History of Earth and Animated Nature* (Thetford, 1810), III, p. 282.
15 Reproduced in Kurt G. Bluchel, *Game and Hunting* (Cologne, 1997), p. 268.
16 George Gascoigne, *The Noble Art of Venerie or Hunting* (London, 1575), quoted in John Layard, *The Lady of the Hare* (London, 1944), p. 204.
17 Robert Burton, *The Anatomy of Melancholy*, ed. Thomas C. Faulkner et al. (Oxford, 1989), I, p. 213.
18 Such beliefs can be traced to a variety of sources, and are summarized in Topsell, *The History of Four-footed Beasts*, pp. 209–10, and John Johnston, *A Description of the Nature of Four-footed Beasts*, pp. 84–6.
19 Thomas Bewick, *A General History of Quadrupeds* (Newcastle upon Tyne, 1790), p. 373.
20 P. H. Gosse, *Natural History: Quadrupeds and Other Mammalia* (London, 1862), p. 226.
21 Charles Darwin, *The Descent of Man* (London, 1890), p. 422.
22 For Darwin's letters see the complete correspondence online at http://darwin.lib.cam.uk, accessed 12 May 2009.
23 Peter Kropotkin, *Mutual Aid: A Factor of Evolution* (London, 1902), pp. 45–6.
24 Claude Lévi-Strauss, quoted in Steve Baker, *Picturing the Beast* (Champaign, IL, 2001), p. 9.
25 Baron Georges Cuvier, *The Animal Kingdom* (London, 1849), p. 118.
26 Philostratus, *Life of Apollonius*, trans. Christopher P. Jones (Cambridge, MA, and London, 2005), 3. 39.
27 Giambattista della Porta, *Naturall Magick* (London, 1658), p. 407.
28 John Aubrey, *Remaines of Gentillisme and Judaisme*, quoted in Layard, *The Lady of The Hare*, p. 105.
29 Ulisse Aldrovandi, *Monstrorum historiae* (Bononiae, 1642), p. 456.
30 F. Edward Hulme, *Natural History Lore and Legend* (London, 1895), p. 79.
31 Ibid., p. 81.

32 Thomas Pennant, *British Zoology* (London, 1768–80), I, p. 87.
33 Ian Niall, *The New Poacher's Handbook* (London, 1960), p. 11.
34 Richard Jefferies, 'The Haunt of the Hare', *The Open Air* (London, 1885), p. 144.
35 Ted Hughes, 'The Hare', *Collected Poems*, ed. Paul Keegan (London, 2003), p. 689.
36 See the report of research by Sarah Williams at news-bio-medicine.org/biology-news-3-/The-Hare-and-the-greyhound-3A-A-race-the-hare-can-win-7378-1, accessed 12 May 2009.
37 'Extract from an unpublished Work on Species', published in 'Three Papers on the Tendency of Species to Form Varieties', *Zoologist*, XVI (1858), pp. 6263–308. The example was later incorporated into *The Origin of Species*, p. 90.
38 B. Grzimek, 'The Hare . . . an Unknown Animal', *Animal Life*, XXX (1965), pp. 19–22.
39 For the account of hare natural history which follows, see the relevant chapters and articles in: Joseph A. Chapman and John E. C. Flux, eds, *Rabbits, Hares and Pikas: Status Survey and Conservation Action Plan* (Gland, 1990); K. Myers and C. D. MacInnes, eds, *Proceedings of the World Lagomorph Conference* (Gland, 1981); Stephen Tapper, *The Brown Hare* (Aylesbury, 1987); K. Myers, I. Parer and B. J. Richardson, 'Leporidae', in D.W.H. Walton and B. J. Richardson, eds, *Fauna of Australia: Vol. 1 B* (Canberra, 1989) pp. 917–31; William Gidley, 'The Lagomorphs, an Independent Order', *Science*, XXXVI/92 (30 August 1912).
40 Mark Twain, *Roughing It* (Berkeley, CA, 1993), pp. 12–13.
41 George Ewart Evans and David Thomson, *The Leaping Hare* (London, 1972), p. 23.
42 Pennant, *British Zoology*, I, p. 87.
43 Charles Darwin, *The Voyage of the 'Beagle'* (London, 1997), p. 51.
44 Evans and Thomson, *The Leaping Hare*, p. 207.
45 William Paley, *Natural Theology* (1802) quoted in Matt Cartmill, *A View to a Death in the Morning* (Cambridge, MA, 1993), pp. 124–5; Herodotus, *The Histories*, trans. Aubrey de Sélincourt (New York, 1972), p. 248.

46 Oppian, *Halieutica*, in *Cynegetica*, trans. A. W. Mair (London, 1928), p. 159.
47 William Cobbett, *Rural Rides* (Harmondsworth, 2001), p. 31.
48 Henry Tegner, *Wild Hares* (Rhyl, 1978).
49 Max Bachrach, *Fur: A Practical Treatise* (London, 1930), p. 189.
50 Quoted in H. A. MacPherson et al, *The Hare* (London, 1896), p. 236.
51 Johnston, *Description of the Nature of Four-footed Beasts*, p. 85.
52 John James Audubon, *Quadrupeds of North America* (Secaucus, NJ, 1989), p. 24.
53 Jean-Anthelme Brillat-Savarin, *The Physiology of Taste* (Harmondsworth, 1994), p. 82.
54 Isabella Beeton, *The Book of Household Management* (Oxford, 2000), p. 238.
55 Quoted in Keith Thomas, *Man and the Natural World* (Harmondsworth, 1983), p. 300.
56 Toby Litt, 'The Hare', in *Best of Young British Novelists 2003* (London, 2003), p. 93.
57 Quoted in Peter Beckford, *Thoughts on Hunting*, ed. Charles Richardson (London, 1947), p. 107.
58 Sir James Frazer, *The Golden Bough* (London, 1936), Pt VII, vol. I, p. 316.
59 *Letters of Ted Hughes*, ed. Christopher Reid (London, 2007), p. 213.
60 Quoted in Ezra Pound, *The Spirit of Romance* (1910), p. 30.
61 See www.traditionalmusic.co.uk/bawdy-songs/001202.HTM, accessed 13 May 2009.
62 Vladimir Nabokov, *Strong Opinions* (New York, 1990), p. 25.
63 See www.newmediastudies.com/art/bordello.htm, accessed 13 May 2009.
64 W. B. Yeats, *The Poems*, ed. Richard J. Finneran (New York, 1989), pp. 136–7.
65 D. H. Lawrence, *Women in Love*, ed. David Farmer et al. (Cambridge, 1987), p. 127.
66 Czesław Miłosz, 'An Encounter', *New and Collected Poems 1931–2001* (London, 2005), p. 27.

67 Wallace Stevens, *Harmonium* (Faber, 2001), p. 56.

68 Evans and Thomson, *The Leaping Hare*, p. 98.

2 MYTHIC HARE

1 Miguel de Cervantes, *Don Quixote*, trans. Charles Jarvis (Oxford, 1998), p. 934.

2 See appendix to George Ewart Evans and David Thomson, *The Leaping Hare* (London, 1972), pp. 202–4, and as translated by Seamus Heaney in *Opened Ground: Poems 1966–1996* (London, 1998), pp. 209–11.

3 Instanced, along with similar superstitions, in C. J. Billson, 'The Easter Hare', *Folk-Lore*, III/4 (December 1892), pp. 440–67.

4 General de Caulaincourt, Duke of Vicenza, *With Napoleon in Russia* (New York, 1995), p. 54.

5 In an unattributed translation quoted in John Layard, *The Lady of the Hare* (Boston, 1988), p. 284.

6 *Homer's 'Iliad'*, trans. Alexander Pope, ed. Theodore Alois Buckley (London, n.d.), p. 398.

7 For this and similar emblems, see the online archive at www.mnemosyne.org, accessed 13 May 2009.

8 *The Oxford Dictionary of English Proverbs*, ed. Joanna Wilson (Oxford, 1970), p. 354.

9 Hans Biedermann, *Dictionary of Symbolism: Cultural Icons and the Meanings Behind Them* (London, 1994), p. 164.

10 Penelope Wilson, *Sacred Signs: Hieroglyphs in Ancient Egypt* (Oxford, 2003), p. 30.

11 E. Wallis Budge, *The Gods of The Egyptians* (Chicago, 1904), I, pp. 27–8.

12 Layard, *The Lady of the Hare*, p. 150.

13 Philostratus, *Imagenes*, quoted in Layard, *The Lady of the Hare*, p. 215.

14 Xenophon, *Memorabilia*, in *Conversations of Socrates*, trans. Robin Waterfield, ed. Hugh Tredennick (London, 1990), pp. 168–9.

15 Layard, *The Lady of the Hare*, p. 194.

16 Jataka no. 322, 'The Sound the Hare Heard', *Jataka Tales of the Buddha, Part III*, trans. Ken and Visakha Kawasaki (Kandy, 1997).
17 William O'Connor, *Folk Tales from Tibet* (London, 1906), pp. 1–5.
18 J. E. Cirlot, *A Dictionary of Symbols* (London, 1962), p. 133.
19 See the article 'Animals in the Bible', in the online *Catholic Encyclopedia* at www.newadvent.org/cathen/01517a.htm, accessed 13 May 2009.
20 Jonathan Sarfati, 'Do Rabbits Chew their Cud? The Bible Beats the Sceptics (Again) . . .', *Creation*, XX/4 (September/November 1998), p. 56.
21 Epistle to Barnabas, ch. 10, www.newadvent.org/fathers/0124.htm.
22 Novatian, 'On the Jewish Meats', www.newadvent.org/fathers/0512.htm.
23 Ibid.
24 St Augustine, *Exposition on the Book of Psalms* (New York, 1847).
25 Richard W. Barber, ed., *Bestiary* (London, 1992), pp. 66–7.
26 Biedermann, *Dictionary of Symbolism*, p. 164.
27 Tertullian, *Scorpiace*, quoted in Geoffrey D. Dunn, *Tertullian* (London, 2004), p. 109.
28 Victoria Salley, *Nature's Artist: Plants and Animals by Albrecht Dürer* (London and New York, 2003), p. 66.
29 In Layard, *The Lady of the Hare*, p. 178.
30 See http://spazioinwind.libero.it/iconografia/Nell.htm, accessed 13 May 2009.
31 See 'The Three Hares Project': www.//chrischapmanphotography.co.uk/hares.
32 M. W. Tisdall, *God's Beasts* (Plymouth, 1998), p. 112.
33 Ibid., p. 114.
34 St Basil, *Hexaemeron*, Homily IX, www.newadvent.org/fathers/32019.
35 St John Chrysostom, 'Homily 7 on *Philippians*', trans. John A. Brodus, in *Nicene and Post-Nicene Fathers*, XIII, ed. Philip Schaff (Buffalo, NY, 1889), p. 153.
36 St Augustine, *City of God*, trans. Henry Bettenson, ed. G. R. Evans (Harmondsworth, 2003), p. 320.

37 Michael Camille, *Image on the Edge: The Margins of Medieval Art* (London, 1992), p. 20.
38 Quoted in ibid., p. 68.
39 Giraldus Cambrensis, *The Historical Works of Giraldus Cambrensis*, ed. Thomas Wright (London, 1863), p. 79.
40 Margaret A. Murray, *The Witch-Cult in Western Europe* (Oxford, 1961), p. 227.
41 W. B. Yeats, *Fairy and Folk Tales of the Irish Peasantry* (London, 1890), pp. 164–5.
42 Robert Chambers, *Domestic Annals of Scotland, from the Reformation to the Revolution* (Edinburgh, 1858), pp. 287–8.
43 Sir Walter Scott, *Letters on Demonology and Witchcraft* (New York, 1848), pp. 224–5.
44 Jeremy Harte, 'Pussy-cat, Pussy-cat, where have you been?', *At The Edge*, VI (May 1997), p. 34.
45 Bernardino de Sahagún, *Historia general de las cosas de Nueva España* III, ed. Carlos Maria de Bustamente (Mexico, 1829), p. 139.
46 Michael Graulich, *Myths of Ancient Mexico* (London, 1977), p. 133.
47 Elizabeth P. Benson, *Birds and Beasts of Ancient Latin America* (Gainsville, FL, 1997), p. 44.
48 Bernard R. Ortiz de Montellano, *Aztec Medicine, Health and Nutrition* (New Brunswick, 1990), p. 180.
49 William Strachey, *Historie of Travell into Virginia Britannia*, quoted in Evans and Thomson, *The Leaping Hare*, p. 130.
50 Paul Radin, *The Winnebago Tribe* (Lincoln, NE, 1970), p. 329.
51 Ruth M. Underhill, *Red Man's Religion* (Chicago and London, 1965), p. 189.
52 For this, and a superb archive including the tales of the hare cycle, see Richard L. Dieterle, 'The Encyclopedia of Hotcak (Winnebago) Mythology' at www.hotcakencyclopedia.com, accessed 14 May 2009.
53 For accounts of African hare-trickster tales, see Philip M. Peck and Kwesi Yankah, *African Folklore: An Encyclopedia* (2004), and O. R. Dathorne, *The Black Mind: A History of African Literature* (Minneapolis, MN, 1974).

54 Ambrose Bierce, *The Devil's Dictionary* (Oxford, 2002), p. 144.
55 Thomas Malthus, *Essay on the Principle of Population* (London, 1826), pp. 290–91.
56 Guy Claxton, *Hare Brain, Tortoise Mind* (London, 1997).
57 *The Fables of Esope, Translated out of Frensshe in to Englysshe by William Caxton* (Newtown, 1931), p. 29.
58 Roger L'Estrange, *Aesop's Fables* (London, 1936), p. 84.
59 Laura Gibbs, *Aesop's Fables* (Oxford, 2002), p. 122.
60 John Layard's *The Lady of the Hare*, first published in London in 1944, began as a case study of a patient who recounted, in course of analysis, an elaborate dream about a hare. Set on the trail of the 'significance' of hares, Layard produced a 120-page essay on 'The Mythology of the Hare' which was then appended to his account of his analysand. Though densely learned, informative and influential, this essay is also significantly shaped and slanted by its author's Jungianism: specifically by the way in which it presents certain sexual and other 'profane' occurrences of the hare in myth as 'decayed' versions of its prior and 'purer' religious significance, or of its primary importance in the 'collective unconscious'.

3 HUNTED HARE

1 Hunting hares with dogs is still legal in Spain, Portugal and Russia. It is illegal in Australia and New Zealand, countries with previously long traditions of hunting hares for sport, and in some parts of the USA. In Ireland enclosed hare coursing continues with the stipulation that the dogs used must be muzzled, enabling the continuance of an annual event as big, perhaps even bigger than the Waterloo Cup. In 2008 its 83rd running in Clonmel, Co. Tipperary, was calculated to have generated up to 16 million euros for the local economy.
2 Xenophon, *Cynegeticus*, ed. and trans. A. A. Phillips and M. M. Willcock, in *Xenophon and Arrian on Hunting* (Warminster, 1999), p. 55.
3 Ibid., p. 53.

4 Ibid., p. 81.
5 Quoted in J.M.C. Toynbee, *Animals in Roman Art and Life* (London, 1973), p. 200.
6 Xenophon, *Cynegeticus*, p. 111.
7 Charlie Pye-Smith, *Hare-Hunting: A Forgotten Field-Sport* (Oakham, 1998), p. 14.
8 Virgil, *Georgics* I, 308, quoted in Toynbee, *Animals in Roman Art and Life*, p. 201.
9 Horace, 'Epistle to Lollius', quoted in J. K. Anderson *Hunting in the Ancient World* (Berkeley, CA, and London, 1985), p. 88.
10 Ovid, *Remedia Amores* 206, quoted in Anderson, *Hunting in the Ancient World*, p. 91.
11 Quoted in John Cummins, *The Hound and the Hawk: The Art of Medieval Hunting* (London, 1998), p. 112.
12 Claude d'Anthenaise, ed., *Il libro della Caccia di Gaston Phebus* (Paris, 2001), pp. 15, 59, 90–94.
13 Edward, Duke of York, *The Master of Game* (London, 1909), pp. 136–46.
14 Dame Juliana Berners, *The Boke of St Albans*, quoted in George Ewart Evans and David Thomson, *The Leaping Hare* (London, 1972), p. 61.
15 George Gascoigne, *The Noble Art of Venerie or Hunting* (London, 1611), p. 162.
16 Peter Beckford, *Thoughts on Hunting*, ed. Charles Richardson (London, 1947), pp. 99–119.
17 Gascoigne, quoted in Edward Berry, *Shakespeare and the Hunt* (Cambridge, 2001), p. 54.
18 Sir Thomas Elyot, *The Book Named the Governour*, ed. S. E. Lehmberg (London, 1962), p. 68.
19 Ben Jonson, *Poems*, ed. Ian Donaldson (Oxford, 1975), p. 92.
20 *Proceedings in Parliament 1610*, vol. I, ed. Elizabeth Read Foster (New Haven, CT, and London, 1966), p. 51.
21 *Anglo-Saxon Chronicle*, trans. and ed. Michael Swanton (London, 1998), p. 221.
22 Quoted in Richard Almond, *Medieval Hunting* (Stroud, 2003), p. 93.

23 Quoted in P. B. Munsche, *Gentlemen and Poachers: The English Game Laws, 1671–1831* (Cambridge, 1981), p. 11.
24 Thomas Carlyle, *The French Revolution,* quoted in Harry Hopkins, *The Long Affray* (London, 1985), p. 285.
25 For game laws in the following summary, see: Munsche, *Gentlemen and Poachers*; Roger B. Manning, *Hunters and Poachers: A Social and Cultural History of Unlawful Hunting in England, 1485–1640* (Oxford, 1993); 'The Hare and the Lawyers' by H. A. MacPherson in *The Hare* (London, 1896), pp. 49–62.
26 Douglas Alexander Stewart and Nancy Keesing, eds, *The Pacific Book of Bush Ballads* (Sydney, 1967), p. 4.
27 Quoted in Munsche, *Gentlemen and Poachers,* p. 88.
28 John Purlevent, *A Dialogue between Lawyer and a Country Gentleman upon the Subject of the Game Laws relative to Hares, Partridges and Pheasants* (London, 1771), p. 42.
29 MacPherson, 'The Hare and the Lawyers', p. 58.
30 Hopkins, *The Long Affray*, p. 206.
31 Ibid., p. 154.
32 Louisa Mary Cresswell, *Eighteen Years on Sandringham Estate* (London, 1887), p. 56.
33 Quoted in Evans and Thomson, *The Leaping Hare,* pp. 250–52.
34 William Shakespeare, *The Narrative Poems,* ed. Maurice Evans (Harmondsworth, 1989), p. 90.
35 Michel de Montaigne, *The Essays*, trans. John Florio (Menston, 1969), p. 249.
36 Quoted in Matt Cartmill, *A View to a Death in the Morning* (Cambridge, MA, 1993), p. 77.
37 Quoted in Keith Thomas, *Man and the Natural World* (London, 1983), pp. 161–2.
38 Ibid., p. 163.
39 Margaret Cavendish, 'The Hunting of the Hare', in Alastair Fowler, ed., *The New Oxford Book of Seventeenth Century Verse* (Oxford, 1991), p. 636.
40 Alexander Pope, *Poetical Works*, ed. Herbert Davis (Oxford, 1966), p. 41.

41 Ibid., p. 40.
42 William Somervile, extract from 'The Chase', in Roger Lonsdale, ed., *The New Oxford Book of Eighteenth Century Verse* (Oxford, 1984), p. 206.
43 David Perkins, 'Cowper's Hares', *Eighteenth Century Literature*, xx/2 (May 1996), pp. 57–69.
44 James Thomson, *Poetical Works*, ed. J. Logie Robertson (Oxford, 1908), p. 147.
45 *The Poems of John Gay*, ed. John Underhill (London, 1893), I, p. 25.
46 Richard Jago, *Edge-Hill, or, the Rural Prospect delineated and moralized* (London, 1767).
47 *The Complete Poetry and Prose of William Blake*, ed. David V. Erdman (New York, 1988), p. 490.
48 *The Poetical Works of Robert Burns*, ed. John Francis Smith (New York, 1865), pp. 177–8.
49 Quoted in Keith Thomas, *Man and The Natural World*, p. 177.
50 'We are moved most by the distressful cries of those animals that have any similitude to the human voice, such as the fawn, and the hare when seized by dogs.' Thomas Sheridan, *A Course of Lectures on Elocution* (London, 1762), p. 104.
51 See www.defra.gov.uk/rural/hunting/inquiry/evidence2/amhbmbhanccalc.htm, accessed 14 May 2009.
52 Anon., *The Hare, or, Hunting Incompatible with Humanity* (Philadelphia, PA, 1802), p. 10.
53 Charles Dickens, *Hard Times*, ed. Paul Schlicke (Oxford, 1989), p. 11.
54 *The Complete Illustrated Lewis Carroll*, with an introduction by Alexander Woollcott (London, 1996), pp. 418–19.

4 PAINTED AND PLASTIC HARE

1 William Shakespeare, *Henry V*, ed. J. H. Walter (London, 1960), III.i, p. 59.
2 *The Works of Lord Byron*, ed. E. H. Coleridge (London, 1900), II, p. 317. In Dryden's coded, politico-religious beast fable 'The Hind

and the Panther', the timorous, 'quaking' hare is used to refer unflatteringly to the Quakers, punning on their pacifism.

3 Heinrich Wölfflin, *The Art of Albrecht Dürer* (London, 1971), p. 142.
4 Fritz Koreny, *Albrecht Dürer and the Animal and Plant Studies of the Renaissance*, trans. Pamela Marwood and Yehuda Shapiro (Boston, MA, 1988).
5 Hans Burgkmair's *John the Evangelist on Patmos* of 1518, reproduced, along with the other main Renaissance imitations and adaptations of Dürer's hare in Koreny, *Albrecht Dürer and the Animal and Plant Studies of the Renaissance*, pp. 132–49.
6 Reproduced in *the photographed animal: useful, cute and collected* (Göttingen, 2005), p. 17.
7 Paul Münch, 'Changing German Perceptions of the Historical Role of Albrecht Dürer', in Dagmar Eichberger and Charles Zika, eds, *Dürer and his Culture* (Cambridge, 1998), p. 181.
8 Wölfflin, *Art of Albrecht Dürer*, p. 142.
9 Anja-Franziska Eichler, *Albrecht Dürer* (Cologne, 1999), p. 135.
10 Richard Jefferies, *The Open Air* (London, 1885), p. 145.
11 Scott A. Sullivan, *The Dutch Game Piece* (Woodbridge, Suffolk, 1984), p. 34.
12 Pierre Rosenberg et al., *Chardin* (New York, 2000), p. 114.
13 Robert Hughes, *Nothing If Not Critical* (London, 1990) p. 76.
14 Sarah R. Cohen, 'Chardin's Fur: Painting, Materialism, and the Question of Animal Soul', *Eighteenth Century Studies*, XXXVIII/1 (Fall 2004), pp. 39–61.
15 Rosenberg, *Chardin*, p. 166.
16 Esti Dunow et al., eds, *Chaim Soutine: A Catalogue Raisonné of the Paintings* (Cologne, 2001), p. 16.
17 Norman L. Kleebatt and Kenneth E. Silver, 'Reading Soutine, Retrospectively', in Kleebatt and Silver, eds, *An Expressionist in Paris: The Paintings of Chaim Soutine* (New York, 1998), pp. 15–16.
18 Heiner Stachelhaus, *Joseph Beuys*, trans. David Britt (New York, 1991), p. 135.
19 Ibid., p. 59.
20 Quoted in Max Reithmann, 'In the Rubblefield of German

History', in Gene Ray, ed., *Joseph Beuys: Mapping the Legacy* (New York, 2001), p. 153.

21 Quoted in Caroline Tisdall, *Joseph Beuys* (London, 1979), p. 101.

22 *The Poems of Paul Celan*, trans. Michael Hamburger (London, 1988), p. 63.

23 Quoted in Steve Baker, *The Postmodern Animal* (London, 2000), p. 62.

24 Interview with Martin Gayford, *Daily Telegraph*, 12 May 2005.

25 Quoted by Angelina Davydova, 'Death Becomes Her', *The St Petersburg Times*, Friday, 3 December 2004.

5 HARE POETRY, HARE THOUGHT

1 *The Compact Edition of the Oxford English Dictionary*, I, p. 1257.

2 Christopher Marlowe, *Complete Works*, ed. Fredson Bowers (Cambridge, 1981), II, p. 450.

3 William Shakespeare, *The Merchant of Venice*, I.ii, in *The Complete Works of William Shakespeare*, ed. W. J. Craig (Oxford, 1978), p. 194.

4 Laurence Sterne, *The Life and Opinions of Tristram Shandy, Gentleman* (Harmondsworth, 2003), p. 194.

5 James Joyce, *Finnegans Wake* (Harmondsworth, 1999), p. 118

6 John Layard, *The Lady of the Hare* (London, 1944), p. 197.

7 Edward Topsell, *The Historie of the Foure-footed Beasts* (London, 1658), p. 141.

8 Karl Josef Höltgen, 'Clever dogs and nimble spaniels: on the iconography of logic, invention and imagination': see http://webdoc.gwdg.de/edoc/ia/eese/artic20/hoeltgen/10_2000.html, accessed 15 May 2009.

9 John Berger, 'The Soul and the Operator', *Keeping a Rendezvous* (London, 1992), p. 231.

10 R. Gray, ed., *Kafka, a Collection of Critical Essays* (1962), pp. 34–5.

11 Eliot Weinberger, 'Next stop, Forbidden City', *London Review of Books*, 23 June 2005.

12 My translation. For the poem in Middle English see George Ewart

Evans and David Thomson, *The Leaping Hare* (London, 1972), pp. 202–4.

13 William Langland, *The Vision of Piers Plowman*, ed. A.V.C. Schmidt (London, 1978), p. 78.

14 *The Complete Works of Geoffrey Chaucer*, ed. Walter W. Skeat (Oxford, 1973), pp. 421, 190–92.

15 See appendix to Evans and Thomson, *The Leaping Hare*, p. 248.

16 Ibid., pp. 250–2.

17 William Shakespeare, *The Narrative Poems*, ed. Maurice Evans (Harmondsworth, 1989), p. 90.

18 Paul Muldoon, *Why Brownlee Left* (London, 1980), p. 18.

19 William Cowper, *The Task: A Poem. In Six Books* (London, 1810), pp. 81–2.

20 *The Poems of William Cowper*, ed. John D. Baird and Charles Ryskamp (Oxford, 1995), pp. 19–20.

21 *The Complete Nonsense of Edward Lear*, ed. Holbrook Jackson (London, 1947), p. 200.

22 *The New Oxford Book of Romantic Period Verse*, ed. Jerome J. Mc Gann (Oxford, 1993), pp. 259–63.

23 *Selected Poems and Prose of John Clare*, ed. Eric Robinson and Geoffrey Summerfield (Oxford, 1967), p. 89.

24 *The Natural History Prose Writings of John Clare*, ed. Margaret Grainger (Oxford, 1983), p. 174.

25 *The Poems of Emily Dickinson*, ed. R. W. Franklin (Cambridge, MA, 1999), p. 48.

26 Guillaume Apollinaire, *Selected Poems*, trans. Oliver Bernard (London, 1986), p. 69.

27 Arthur Rimbaud, *A Season in Hell and Illuminations*, trans. Mark Treharne (London, 1998), p. 55.

28 David Harsent's sequence 'Lepus' appears in his *Marriage* (London, 2002), his 'The Woman and the Hare' in *Legion* (London, 2005); his libretto for Harrison Birtwhistle with the Nash Ensemble's 2002 recording *The Woman and the Hare* (Black Box, BBM 1046, 2002). John Kinsella uses Sidney Nolan's 'Hare in Trap' on the cover of *The Hunt* (Newcastle upon Tyne, 1998);

Pisanello's hare appears on the cover of Pauline Stainer's *The Lady and the Hare: New and Selected Poems* (Newcastle upon Tyne, 2003); the image reproduced on page 128 of this book is used for the cover of Bernard O'Donoghue's *Outliving* (London, 2003). For T. S. Eliot see Christopher Ricks, ed., *Inventions of the March Hare, Poems 1909–1917* (London, 1996). Paul Muldoon's hares include the hunted one encountered in his poem 'Beagles', in *Moy Sand and Gravel* (London, 2002): 'looking as/ if he might for a moment put/ himself in my place, thinking better of it, sloping off/ behind the lorry-bed.' For a radically alternative, non-naturalistic recent poetic take on the hare, see Valerio Magrelli's sequence 'The Duck-Hare Individual' in *The Embrace: Selected Poems*, trans. Jamie McKendrick (London, 2009), pp. 98–109.

29 Ted Hughes 'The Warm and the Cold', in *Collected Poems*, ed. Paul Keegan (London, 2003), p. 343.

30 Hughes, *Collected Poems*, pp. 687–90.

Select Bibliography

Anderson, J. K., *Hunting in the Ancient World* (Berkeley, CA, and London, 1985)
Aria, Cesar, *The Hare*, trans. Nick Caistor (London, 1998)
Anon., *The Hare, or, Hunting Incompatible with Humanity* (Philadelphia, 1802)
d'Anthenaise, Claude, ed., *Il libro della Caccia di Gaston Phebus* (Paris, 2001)
Benson, Elizabeth, *Birds and Beasts of Latin America* (Gainesville, FL, 1997)
Berry, Edward, *Shakespeare and the Hunt* (Cambridge, 2001)
Billson, C. J., 'The Easter Hare', *Folk-Lore*, III/4 (December 1892), pp. 440–66
Blüchel, Kurt G., *Game and Hunting* (Cologne, 1997)
Browne, Sir Thomas, *Pseudodoxia Epidemica* (London, 1858)
Bryden, H. A., *Hare-hunting and Harriers* (London, 1903)
Camille, Michael, *Image on the Edge: The Margins of Medieval Art* (London, 1992)
Cartmill, Matt, *A View to a Death in the Morning: Hunting and Nature Through History* (Cambridge, MA, 1993)
Chapman, Joseph A., and John E. C. Flux, eds, *Rabbits, Hares and Pikas: Status Survey and Conservation Action Plan* (Gland, 1990)
Cummins, John, *The Hound and The Hawk: The Art of Medieval Hunting* (London, 1998)
Evans, George Ewart, and David Thomson, *The Leaping Hare* (London, 1972)

Gidley, William, 'The Lagomorphs an Independent Order', *Science*, xxxvi/92 (August 1912)
Hewitt, William Lovell, *Hare Hunting* (London, 1975)
Hopkins, Harry, *The Long Affray: The Poaching Wars in Britain* (London, 1986)
Johnston, John, *A Description of the Nature of Four-footed Beasts*, trans. 'J. P.' (Amsterdam, 1678)
Kingdon, Jonathan, *East African Mammals: Hares and Rodents* (Chicago, 1984)
Koreny, Fritz, *Albrecht Dürer and the Animal and Plant Studies of the Renaissance*, trans. Pamela Marwood and Yehuda Shapiro (Boston, MA, 1988)
Koslow, Susan, *Frans Snyders: The Noble Estate: Seventeenth Century Still-Life and Animal Painting in the Southern Netherlands* (Antwerp, 1995)
Layard, John. *The Lady of The Hare* (London, 1944)
Leclerc, Georges Louis, Comte de Buffon, *Natural History, General and Particular*, trans. William Smellie (London, 1812)
Litt, Toby, 'The Hare', *Best of Young British Novelists* 2003 (London, 2003)
MacPherson, Rev. H. A., et al., *The Hare* (London, 1896)
Manning, Roger B., *Hunters and Poachers: A Social and Cultural History of Unlawful Hunting in England,* 1485–1640 (Oxford, 1993)
Mason, Jill, *The Hare* (Ludlow, 2005)
Mezzalira, Francesco, *Bestie e Bestiari* (Turin, 2001)
Munsche, P. B., *Gentlemen and Poachers: the English Game Laws,* 1671–1831 (Cambridge, 1981)
Myers, K., and C. D. MacInnes, eds, *Proceedings of the World Lagomorph Conference* (Gland, 1981)
Paullini, Franz Christian, *Lagographia Curiosa* (Schöningen, 1691)
Perkins, David, 'Cowper's Hares', *Eighteenth Century Literature*, xx/2 (May 1996), pp. 57–69
Phillips, A. A. and Willcock, M. M., eds, *Cynegeticus: Xenophon and Arrian on Hunting* (Warminster, 1999)
Pye-Smith, Charlie, *Hare-hunting: A Forgotten Field Sport* (Oakham, 1998)

Radin, Paul, *The Trickster: A Study in American Indian Mythology* (New York, 1972)
Rosenberg, Pierre, ed., *Chardin* (London, 2000)
Schirmer, Lothar, ed., *Essential Joseph Beuys* (London, 1996)
Syson, Luke, and Gordon Dillian, eds, *Pisanello* (London, 2001)
'"Tantara" (A Master of Harriers)', *Hare Hunting* (London, 1893)
Tapper, Stephen, *The Brown Hare* (Aylesbury, 1987)
Tegner, Henry, *Wild Hares* (Rhyl, 1969)
Thomas, Keith, *Man and The Natural World* (London, 1983)
Topsell, Edward, *The Historie of the Foure-footed Beasts* (London, 1658)
Toynbee, J.M.C., *Animals in Roman Art and Life* (London, 1973)
Waldung, Wolfgang, *Lagographia* (Amberg, 1619)
Wyn Hughes, D., ed., *Hares* (London, 1981)

Associations & Websites

UKALIQ: THE ARCTIC HARE

www.nature.ca/ukaliq
Canadian site, including photos and video footage, looking at Arctic hares 'from biological cultural and scientific points of view'

LAGOMORPH SPECIALIST GROUP

www.ualberta.ca/~dhik/lsg/ARCHIVE.HTM
Website detailing specialist, scientific publications and conferences relating to all lagomorphs

BURNS INQUIRY

www.huntinginquiry.gov.uk
Site containing documents relating to the 2004 ban on hunting with dogs in England and Wales, with information on the history and contemporary status of hare hunting, as well as oral testimony from pro-hunting lobbyists

ACTION PLAN FOR THE BROWN HARE

www.ukbap.org.ukplans.aspx?ID=410
Outline of the scheme to promote hare ecology in the UK

JACKALOPES AND HORNED HARES

www.lafayette.edu/~hollidac/jackalope
Site devoted to the curious popularity of 'jackalopes' (faked jackrabbit/ deer hybrids) in the United States, with a history of their legendary European cousins

THREE HARES PROJECT

www.threehares.net
Site devoted to investigations into the significance of the three hares motif in Europe, Asia and the Middle East, with useful links, especially to http://chrischapmanphotopraphy.com/hares/index.html

WIKIPEDIA HARE

http://en.wikipedia.org/wiki/Hare
Online encyclopedia entry with useful links and information on hare species

Acknowledgements

Thanks to Jonathan Burt, the series editor, for encouragement and detailed engagement with the final typescript; to Rebecca Stott for first suggesting that I contribute to the 'Animal' series. To Phil Baker for an appreciation of 'Lagographia Curiosa'; to Jamie McKendrick for many suggestions. To Michael Leaman at Reaktion Books for being still at the finishing-line, long after the tortoise had crossed it. Above all to Erica Segre. 'Hare Writing' was first published in the *Times Literary Supplement*.

Photo Acknowledgements

The author and publishers wish to express their thanks to the below sources of illustrative material and/or permission to reproduce it:

Akg-Images: pp. 63 (Erich Lessing), 67 (Erich Lessing), 144 (Erich Lessing), 198 (Erich Lessing); © The Estate of Francis Bacon. All rights reserved. DACS 2009: pp. 158, 159; © DACS 2009: pp. 160, 164, 166, 168, 170; The Canadian Museum of Nature: p.31 (right); Con Finlay: p. 31 (left); © Barry Flanagan, courtesy Waddington Galleries, London: pp. 171, 194; Getty Images: pp. 121, 196; Istockphoto: p. 33 (dpriebe1); Rex Features: pp. 35 (Andy Rouse), 116 (Richard Austin), 118 (Fotex), 122 (Chris Bourchier), 123 (Simon Roberts); Harry Scott: p. 192; Marty Souffer Productions Ltd: p. 38; © Francisco Toledo. DACS, 2009: pp. 173, 174, 183; The Wellcome Trust Ltd: p. 18; Werner Forman Archive: pp. 66 (top), 83; Courtesy White Cube: p. 175.

Index